LEARNING TO BE

Learning To Be

The Education of Human Potential

JOHN MANN

The Free Press, New York

Collier–Macmillan Limited, London

The Free Press
A Division of The Macmillan Company
866 Third Avenue, New York, New York 10022

Collier–Macmillan Canada Ltd., Toronto, Ontario

Library of Congress Catalog Card Number:
73–143524

printing number
1 2 3 4 5 6 7 8 9 10

To The Students Who Are Waiting

CONTENTS

PREFACE

During the past decade there has been a remarkable development of educational alternatives: open classrooms, free schools, experimental schools, store front schools, and the like. These experiments have been conducted both within and outside of formal education. Their variety is bewildering, but they share a number of common themes.

First, teachers have become more like guides and less like instructors, in schools which stress the freedom of the individual to follow his own interests rather than stretch or shrink him to fit the demands of an externally imposed curriculum.

The curriculum too has been redefined. The variety of offerings has been expanded. The clearest example is the free school where anyone can start courses ranging from witchcraft to flower arranging, if he can find students to enroll in them.

Further, interest has shifted from content to process. Traditional teaching emphasizes mastering a specified content. If the material is learned, the process is more or less irrelevant, though certain techniques such as lectures, text books, and standardized tests are traditionally utilized. In contrast, process instruction teaches the individual how to use the resources at his disposal. When these are mastered, he is able to apply them to content areas that are personally or socially relevant.

Another trend has been to bring together the classroom

and the community. There are "schools without walls" such as the Parkway School in Philadelphia where the activities take place throughout the community. Other schools are using community resources more than in the past. Programs of foreign study and travel also fall into this category, though they emphasize contact with unfamiliar cultures rather than practical experiences with the social forces molding the local environment.

To reduce these innovations to their simplest common denominator, they emphasize the personal growth of the individual as the heart of the educational experience, whereas more traditional approaches place first priority on the transmission of information. This distinction is clouded because most educational theorists, regardless of their persuasion, emphasize the rounded development of the individual within the context of social need. The difference then is not so much in conception as is practice. The traditionalist emphasizes almost totally mastering the intellectual content of specialized subject matter. The experimentalist helps the individual to understand his own capacities and how to utilize them. The subject matter becomes material on which the individual develops his own skills rather than something he is exposed to by those who presumably know what is good for him.

It is not the purpose of this book to describe or analyze recent educational experimentation or the criticism which it has generated. For those interested in such material a number of volumes can be recommended.[1] It is rather to describe a comprehensive alternative which draws from both traditional and progressive approaches and reaches beyond either toward an educational experience in which the goal is to teach the student how to *understand, direct,* and *develop* himself. The purpose of such an educational experience is to aid the individual to cultivate his capabilities, through self-study, skill training, and a variety of behavior change experiences. It is process-oriented. On the other hand, such a goal cannot realistically be attained unless it is systematically pursued within the context of an identifiable curriculum, which, however responsive to individual differences, provides a framework upon which the individual can rely for support. In this respect it is traditional in intent. For purposes of discussion this will be described as the "Internal Curriculum," because it combines humanistic emphasis with systematic training.

If the focus of the educational experience is placed on helping the individual to understand, direct, and develop his own organism, what does this involve? First, we must provide some categories in terms of which the organism can be described and analyzed. The selection of these categories depends not so much on the usual criteria of precision or equivalence as on their usefulness in reducing a vague concept, such as "the human organism," into terms for which precise methods can be designed and applied.

We must also identify known methods by which these human functions can be approached, controlled, and cultivated. Such methods exist, but for the most part they have been developed outside of educational contexts. The recent development of growth centers throughout the United States has helped to generate an increasing awareness of their existence, but this awareness has been obscured by the sensational emphasis that such centers have been given in the mass media.[2]

Further, we must describe how these methods can be related to existing educational practices. Within these pages fifteen human functions will be discussed, methods for cultivating these functions will be described, and applications of these methods to traditional subject matter will be suggested. In addition, we will assess the practicality of an internal curriculum devoted to the cultivation of these functions.

Many examples will be given to illustrate how each function relates to concrete problems and challenges that any teacher must resolve. It is important to understand the spirit and purpose of these examples. Few of the procedures given in the examples have been scientifically validated. They vary in the degree of sophistication and preparation required by the teacher for their proper application. It is best to view these examples as idealized situations that indicate what is possible once both teachers and students are more open to experimentation. If the teacher chooses to apply these procedures, it should be done in a spirit of caution and with an awareness of the degree of openness and acceptance existing within the school system in which he functions. None of the methods that are presented are guaranteed to work automatically. Some require specialized skills that can be obtained or fortified only by attending workshops and other human relations experiences. Many innovations are spread by interested people who simply take what they have heard about in such workshops and try it out for themselves.

A number of the methods that I shall suggest, particularly in the areas of creativity, environmental reorganization, and social-emotional expression, are currently being applied in schools, experimental colleges, and other innovative educational settings. Descriptions of two educational experiments that most nearly approximate the approaches of this book have been published. The first, *Reach, Touch and Teach: Student Concerns and Process Education,* by Terry Borton, describes a set of educational experiences designed to develop the capacities of urban slum children through teaching processes of understanding and development of an intellectual, social, and physical character.[3] The second is *Human Teaching for Human Learning,* by George Brown.[4] This book describes a project sponsored by the Ford Foundation and designed to translate the work on human potential organized and applied at the Esalen Institute, Big Sur, California to the training of public school teachers. These works are forerunners in the area of application, just as this book is a herald of a new possibility in educational design. They can be sensed like a change in the wind, whose direction can be detected but whose outer limits cannot be drawn.

J.M.

LEARNING TO BE

PART I ‖ *Processes for Educating Human Potential*

CHAPTER ONE

SENSING THE HUMAN ORGANISM

OUR sensations are the grounding of our experience. If we are unaware of warmth and cold, tension and relaxation, of our orientation in space, the pull of gravity, the
placement of our legs, arms, trunk, the vibration in our chest
and neck when we talk; then in a fundamental sense we are
unaware of ourselves.

There are three major approaches to cultivating the
awareness of sensations. The simplest involves focusing on
"that which is." This approach is found in its purest form in
the work originated fifty years ago by Elsa Gindler and Hein-
rich Jacoby. It is only recently that Charlotte Selver, the principal authority on this approach in the United States, has
written the first brief statement about the work that is widely
available.[1] As she describes it, this approach has consisted of
nothing more than being aware of sensations as they occur,
making no effort to change them. One becomes an alert observer. Although this sounds childishly simple, it is somewhat
like advising a person going horseback riding for the first
time that all he has to do is stay on the horse. The question is
"How?" One does not create in a few days the inner sensitiv-

ity that is required. It is, however, relatively easy to get a taste of the approach.

The questions below, if read slowly, will give you some impression of what is involved. Each question should be viewed as a sip of wine or a morsel of food. One takes it in, savors it, swallows it, and then is ready for the next. It is characteristic of the approach that questions are asked, rather than statements made. If you wish to test its effectiveness, ask yourself the following questions in a leisurely fashion, allowing about five seconds to elapse between questions.

Do you have any awareness that you are present in a room reading a book?

Do you have any sense of the weight of your body?

Can you sense where your body contacts the chair (or the floor)?

Can you allow the chair (or the floor) to hold you up?

Are there any places in your body that are particularly tense?

If you attend to the places that are tense, what effect does that have?

If you attend to a place that is relaxed, what effect does that have?

Are you aware of anything moving inside you?

Do you sense the beating of your own heart?

Can you sense the blood beating in the arteries around your body?

Can you sense movement in your eyes and eyelids?

Are you aware of your breathing? Is it shallow or deep? Does becoming aware of your breathing change it in any way?

This work is very gentle. It consists of aiding the student to discover the operation of his own organism by directing his attention to his sensations in a nonjudgmental manner.

A second approach to increasing sensory awareness involves external manipulation of the body. These external actions may involve slapping, tapping, stroking, or massage, all of which are essentially pleasant experiences, or in contrast painful manipulation of tissues designed to restore proper functioning to muscles that are imbalanced, tense or disused.

The major aspect common to these manipulations is that after the intervention from the outside, the person re-experiences "that which is" and is able to realize from his own experience that he is capable of more enjoyable and vivid sensations than he had believed possible. One of the persons who has developed such methods is Bernard Gunther of the Esalen Institute. One of his introductory sessions might consist of the following experiences which you can try for yourself.

1. Stand quietly and relaxed. If possible, be barefoot. Take a moment to sense how your body feels.
2. Shake yourself as you might shake a rag doll. Sense what that does to you.
3. Starting at the top of your head, perform the following actions. Tap your skull. Your fingers should be slightly bent at the joints. The tapping should feel like gentle rain. You should maintain an awareness of your fingertips as you tap. After finishing the top of your head; shift to the back; then go above the ears and finally to the forehead. Tap in each area about ten seconds. When you are done, go back over any area that feels as though it could use more. Then stand quietly and experience how your head feels.
4. Next work on your face, using gentle slaps. Start at your cheeks, then your chin, under your chin, gently around the lips, the nose, and very gently around the eyes. Spend about ten seconds in each area. When you have finished, go back over any area that seems to need more stimulation. Then stand quietly and experience how your face feels.

In this manner go over the whole body, bringing it to life area by area. The effect is particularly noticeable when working with the limbs. Try the following: Extend the right arm in a relaxed manner. Using the left hand, slap the right arm beginning at the right hand and going up to the shoulder. Be firm. Go over the front, the back, and both sides of the arm. Do it several times. When you have finished, stand quietly with your eyes shut and experience the arm you have worked on. How does it feel compared to the other arm? If the difference is great, carry out the same process on the left arm.

The purpose of the touching, tapping, and slapping is to help to stimulate the body so that the sensations it provides are more vivid. This is not physical education. The goal is not to develop the body but to increase one's experience of it. These methods have been graphically described and photographed in Gunther's books.[2]

Various Hindu and Buddhist teachings provide a third approach to the cultivation of sensations. One of the most striking documents relating to the cultivation of awareness is found in an early Buddhist scripture translated as "Setting Up Mindfulness."[3] In essence this teaching states that the aspirant must be aware of whatever he is doing. If he breathes, he is aware of it. If he pauses, he is aware of it. If he sits, stands, lies down, he is aware of it. If he talks, he is aware of it. The basic concept is similar to those already described. What is different is that it occurs in a foreign culture in a system designed to perfect and expand conscious experience. The founders of Buddhism placed great emphasis on awareness of sensation as the foundation on which a profound self-understanding could be built.

This orientation finds a more concrete form in the Zen Buddhist practice of *Kinhin*, a form of walking meditation. During this process, the individual focuses his attention on his breathing. He holds his hands in a certain posture and walks according to a prescribed gait and speed. The purpose is to help the individual strengthen his ability to control his attention and focus it on his own inner state under conditions that are more difficult than mere sitting. Again, the cultivation of sensation is used as an approach to the eventual alteration of consciousness. Without worrying about the fine points of the technique, it might interest you to put down the book, stand up, focus your attention on your breathing, and begin to walk slowly around the room to gain some sense of the process involved.

Educational Applications*

One useful application of sensory awareness techniques to education is in the resolution of tense or difficult situations. Such events may arise from a variety of causes ranging from intense intellectual concentration, emotional outbursts against discipline in the classroom, or simply continuous effort involving relatively uninteresting material.

A second application involves the use of sensory awareness techniques as an aid in approaching materials viewed as threatening by the student. Everyone finds certain subjects difficult. Unfortunately, when difficulties occur, the tension and anxiety that become associated with the subject grow out of proportion and interfere with the learning process itself. One approach to breaking out of this vicious circle is to train the student to be more sensitive to the patterns of tension that occur when he approaches the material of which he is afraid. This involves experiencing the pain, rather than avoiding or denying it.

A series of questions can help him to become more aware of the location, quality and intensity of his discomfort; such as "Where do you feel most tense?" "Do you experience different kinds of tension in different places in your body?" "Does becoming aware of the tension make it worse or allow it to ease?"

A final application of sensory awareness methods is in overcoming barriers to integrating any difficult material. In many problem-solving endeavors there is a stage at which further effort is fruitless. At such moments the best thing one can do is relax and allow the creative process to go on uncon-

* For this and other human functions there are only a limited number of classroom applications that are possible. Repetition is unavoidable. Thus, one can approach the problem of student restlessness through a variety of different methods emphasizing sensation, movement, emotional expression, or role performance. Each might be effective but for different reasons.

On the other hand certain exercises are uniquely related to certain educational situations. For example, if the student's reaction to the teacher as teacher is interfering with the learning process, role reversal (allowing the student to be teacher) may be the most effective approach. But an ideal fit of technique to event is rare.

sciously. Continued effort leads only to discouragement, tension, and anxiety. At such moments a series of questions can help the individual to relax sufficiently to allow a solution to emerge. The questions given on page 4 can be adopted as a tentative format for such an approach.

Sensory Awareness and the Internal Curriculum

Beyond the educational applications of sensory awareness, or any of the following 14 human functions, is the broader issue of their implications for the reform of educational experience. Each of these functions, with the exception of intellectual capacity, is partially or totally ignored in most educational programs. Therefore a simple point of departure in developing an educational experience devoted to teaching the individual how to understand, control, and develop his total organism would be to have courses devoted to the cultivation of each of these human functions. In a preliminary sense they might constitute the Internal Curriculum.

Let us start with sensory awareness. Can a course be given in this subject? Is there sufficient material? Does this subject relate to the principle of understanding, directing, and developing the human organism? The answer to these questions is "yes." Such courses are currently available in locations throughout the country.

Perhaps the more crucial question is whether sensory awareness is important enough to justify devoting time to its cultivation. Sensory awareness helps to provide us with the grounding of our experience. Our body is the intervening variable in every action we perform. If we are not acquainted with it and do not relate to it as we move through our daily routine, there is something wrong with our relation to ourselves and everything we touch.

But what would a person gain as the result of a course in this area that he would not have without it? If he took a course in organic chemistry, the content of his understanding could be defined beforehand. There is no definable content of sensory awareness except the awareness itself, which is constantly shifting. The content consists of the methods for cultivating physical awareness that the student learns and can apply to himself when he is not in class.

In any form of training there are two distinct aspects. The first is the group experience in which a leader guides the class. This is relatively easy because the situation is created to maximize the likelihood of understanding and success. The second aspect is the work the individual does when he is by himself. The pianist practices his scales; the artist sketches. The student of sensory awareness learns to increase his awareness of his organism in the midst of daily activities he is called on to perform—walking, sitting, eating, sleeping, talking, working, playing. He takes what he experiences in the class and integrates it into his patterns of behavior. This is the homework of such a class. It involves experimentation to determine which methods work best in given circumstances. It involves some form of record keeping and analysis. It may involve group discussion and evaluation of individual results.

How can a process be evaluated? It seems a contradiction in terms. Evaluation is quantitative, fixed. It cannot, on the face of it, be related to a shifting experience. Nevertheless, when a person becomes steeped in his own sensations, it affects everything he does, how he looks, how he moves, how he responds to words and how he uses them. All this is visible, particularly to the trained eye. An effective teacher of sensory awareness has little difficulty in evaluating the degree of progress of the student even though he cannot rely on objective means, such as multiple choice testing. This evaluating ability is a vital part of the teaching skill. Unless the teacher can sense something of the inner experience of the student, he cannot tell what the student needs. Learning and evaluating are closely related although they can be separated for purposes of recording progress.

The notion of marking may seem inappropriate to the

theory of personal growth, but feedback is one of the most effective methods of changing behavior. Marks of an appropriate kind are a form of feedback and need not be eliminated. The opinions and assessment of others help us determine the significance of our own actions.

The fundamental principle underlying sensory awareness practice is that the body contains a source of wisdom that we ignore. It knows how to function and experience, but our personality and beliefs interfere with our hearing and understanding its language. As people grow older, they come to believe that health is the greatest blessing. But this is only a partial truth. Health is valued when it is lost. A greater benediction is to experience and appreciate normal functioning while it exists. It is toward this end that the cultivation of sensory awareness is directed.

CHAPTER TWO

PERCEIVING THE
ENVIRONMENT

L EARNING involves communication. The limiting condition on any communication is the amount of information we can perceive. The cultivation of perceptual awareness is therefore a crucial variable in the educational process.

Perceptual processes are under widespread investigation, particularly comparisons of how the senses function under normal and abnormal circumstances. In contrast, our focus in this book is upon the expansion of normal levels of perceptual awareness. In this area much related work is also being done. For example, students of the reading process have developed methods that enable persons to read faster and with equal or greater comprehension by training them to see more in their eye span. Similar methods have been developed in the field of memory training.

A somewhat different approach to the same problem has been developed in studies of sensory deprivation. In such experiments the individual is deprived of external sensory input. Although the purpose of this work is to study the place of perception in the maintenance of the individual's orientation to his external environment, it may serve as a training

11

device in its own right, helping to focus attention on given stimuli by clearing the mind of familiar perceptual patterns. Recently, for example, a perceptive learning device has been developed that attempts to wipe clean the various distracting impressions that are built up during the day.[1]

Perceptual processes are the basis of any educational experience. Nevertheless, with the exception of training in reading skills, the student is rarely taught how to see, hear, touch, or smell. At best, specialized professional training may emphasize an aspect of a particular sense, such as the use of color in fine arts classes. But in such classes the individual does not so much learn how to see as he is taught what to expect.

Most children know how to see. Perceptual experience hits them with a direct force. Adults do not see directly except under unusual circumstances. Everything adults perceive is filtered through a veil of assumptions, expectations, and distracting thoughts. They are rarely aware of the green grass or the blue sky. They must be taught how to recapture what they have lost in the process of maturation.

Three basic approaches have been developed to enhance perceptual experience. The first of these forces the individual to take in more perceptions by putting him under some pressure, improving his motivation, or stretching his awareness. The second helps him to focus on perceptual details. The third helps him to perceive what is there by eliminating all that is between him and the perception.

Pushing the individual beyond his normal capacity is illustrated by speed-reading practices. The individual is made to read more words at a faster rate. Since this process is relatively familiar, it will not be described here.

In contrast to this stretching approach, one can improve perception by focusing more completely on what is being perceived. An illustration of this orientation is provided by the work of Mouni Sadhu.[2] His essential purpose is the development of concentration, a function which is closely related to willing. However, some of Sadhu's methods utilize perceptions as the object of concentration and are therefore relevant in the present context. His exercises are arranged in order of difficulty, involving both perception and visualization. In the first exercise the individual observes the moving second hand of a watch, noting exactly when he starts and when he loses track of the second hand. When some proficiency has been gained, the individual then observes the head of a pin in as much detail as possible. In a later exercise the student passes from seeing the details of the pin one at a time, to seeing the pin from all sides simultaneously. This requires the power of visualization as well as perception.

This work is often surprisingly difficult to perform. Its purpose is to develop the individual's ability to place his attention where he wishes it to go, to see one thing and shut out the rest. Such training is in harmony with the nature of vision. The eye has one spot of greatest sensitivity. Eye movements help us to see by shifting this spot across the perceptual field. Speed reading emphasizes the expansion of the perceptual field. Sadhu's technique emphasizes sharpening the point of focus. Both are necessary in any systematic training process.

The contrasting approach is to allow perception to take place naturally, by removing the obstacles standing in its way. For this to occur the individual must be in a calm and energetic inner state. Perhaps the clearest description of such an approach, as it relates to the perceptual process, is given by Minor White, a photographer interested not only in taking photographs but also in learning how to look at them.[3] White has identified four stages in the perception of a photograph. The first is "preparation." An appealing photograph is selected and placed in a good light. The individual sits in front of it in a comfortable position and closes his eyes. He then progressively relaxes his body, starting with his eyes and slowly working down toward his legs. This may take four or five minutes. At the end of this period the individual should feel light and full of energy. He waits until this energy seems ready to flow up inside him. As it does, he opens his eyes and attempts to stay aware of his strong initial impression of the photograph.

The second stage of White's approach is "work." This stage is initiated by an increased awareness of the third dimension in the photograph, a greater brilliance of detail, or a deepening of colors or shading. When this has occurred, the individual begins systematically to scan the picture in detail. He utilizes all his technical knowledge to analyze what he sees. At the same time he remains aware of his associations to the picture.

The third stage is the "passive mode," following or substituting for the work period. In it the individual simply remains passive until the picture begins to reach him in some manner. He relaxes and lets the picture talk to him. The success of this approach depends on the inner state of the individual and his willingness to allow impressions to affect him. His effort is not to look but to remain open, without judging either what he sees or his reaction to it.

The fourth stage involves "remembering." The individual takes in a final overall impression of the picture and then closes his eyes. The process of "remembering" the experience is essentially nonverbal. The individual senses what the picture has done to him, the taste it has left in his mouth, the echo in his ear. The remembering process is designed to constitute a bridge between the viewing experience and the normal state of casual observation. It also allows the individual to take some time to integrate his experience with the photograph into his own experience of himself. These four stages may take half an hour or longer to experience and can be performed by a single individual or a small group of persons who share their experiences at the end of the process.

White defines perception differently from Sadhu. To Sadhu, perception is a point of contact. For White it is an experience involving perceptual elements as well as the more subtle overtones of memory, emotion, and the inner experience that the perception stimulates or suggests.

Applications

The most obvious application of perceptual awareness is to teaching aesthetic appreciation. For this purpose one could utilize the approach suggested by Minor White. Although this application is specific in terms of focusing upon a picture, there is no reason that it must be limited to arts classes. A history class might work with a picture that represents a scene from a period they are studying, to help bring the event to life and relate it to their own experience. A chemistry class might focus on a photograph of a crystal as a preparation for studying its more formal characteristics. The possibilities are greater than seem apparent.

A different kind of application of perceptual awareness can occur in relation to study habits. A basic difficulty in successful studying is the maintenance of proper concentration. Breaking up the study period by the occasional application of perceptual concentration as described earlier in relation to Sadhu's work might prove helpful in clearing the mind and restoring needed perspective.

A Class in Perceiving

Perceptual experiences should be varied. For example, the first time Minor White's approach to perceiving might employ a photograph as its focus, the next time music, and the third time a recorded conversation. Each exercise would help to translate the inner conditions required for heightened perception into a new area of experience.

The methods developed by Sadhu for heightening perceptual awareness through concentration form an approach that requires continuous drill if it is to be perfected. Some of this can be done as homework through an appropriate workbook. Some can be done in class directed by the teacher.

Several approaches to the improvement of reading skills are directly concerned with extending the field of visual perception and form the natural complement to work on concentration. Special equipment can be employed to control exposure of visual material and speed of presentation. This work in combination with the work on concentration could occupy a number of sessions.

Psychologists have evolved much useful material in terms of devising methods for standardizing and measuring perceptual differentiations of sight, sound, taste, and other stimuli. These objective distinctions can be used for training purposes. One series of exercises might involve the detection of minimal differences between stimuli that are almost identical in tone, hue, or taste. Another series of comparisons might involve the discrimination between one class of stimuli, such as color, in which only one or more characteristics were varied, holding others constant. Thus, saturation and brightness might vary slightly while hue remained the same. The necessary hardware already exists for providing these kinds of experience.

The next logical step would be to have the students begin to analyze the normal environment. They might search for all examples of a given color within the room and then analyze the difference between examples, distinguishing not only between perceptual qualities but specifying what aspects of the color differed and by approximately how much. They would learn to see color as the student of composition learns to hear music through his understanding of how it is put together. A similar approach can be adopted to other perceptual modalities.

A further approach to the study of perception might utilize the principle of translation. The student would start from a given perception and attempt to translate it into a different medium. This would force him to become more aware of the original perception and of its inherent quality and complexity. Thus, if he has to sing a color or make a poem about a musical composition, he will be forced to listen or see intently as a prelude to such creative effort.

Perhaps heightened awareness would lead the individual to suffer in the modern environment. Color is stark, noise endless, smells and tastes objectionable. The sensitive individual does suffer. The problem, however, is that there are too few sensitive people. If more people tasted, smelled, saw, and heard what was around them, they might not tolerate living in a deteriorating environment.

late a living process in objective mathematical terms realizes how many aspects of that process require further clarification if simulation is to be effective. In the same sense the inadequacies of a performance can lead to a recognition of the need for a deeper understanding of the material.

A Class in Movement

It is not difficult to describe a whole course devoted to movement. Many different courses could be developed independently of each other. The Laban approach can be taught on a regular class basis to various age groups. Similarly, the Mary Whitehouse approach to moving as a means of changing the level of awareness has been adapted to a regular classroom pattern. These approaches are markedly different from each other and from other forms of movement, such as the Japanese martial arts. These arts include archery, swordsmanship, Judo, and more recently, Aikido. Each of these activities requires a lengthy period of instruction. Aikido students, for example, attend classes three times a week for one hour sessions. In order to earn a black belt in such a self-defense system years of practice are required. The purpose of this training is to be able to take any hostile action and reverse the energy flow so that the attacker is floored by the very energy that he had directed against his opponent. This might be viewed as physical nonviolence. The individual initiates nothing, but he is relatively invulnerable because he has learned how to redirect negative forces that seek to injure him. This requires skill and control of attention. It is based on an understanding of how the body moves and how to control its actions.

Another eastern approach is the ancient Hindu discipline of Hatha Yoga. This is a system of physical culture designed to heighten the strength, endurance and general level of health of the organism as a preliminary to more strenuous spiritual ordeals. In recent years classes in Hatha Yoga have become more widely available in large cities, but they have rarely been taught as part of an organized curriculum.

There are many other approaches to the development of the body, some of which are familiar: competitive games, modern and classic dance, and gymnastics. Others, such as the Rolfe method, which involves the painful manipulation of unbalanced and degenerated muscular patterns, are much less well known. The essential point is that moving the body can be a far richer and more complex activity and that there are already available a variety of systematic approaches to help the individual understand, control, and develop this aspect of his functioning.

CHAPTER FOUR

EMOTIONAL EXPRESSION

IT is customary to describe feelings and emotional reactions as belonging to the affective domain. The affective area of experience has long been recognized in educational circles and has served as the object of much analysis.[1] However, the attempt to identify fundamental emotions and trace their developmental patterns is primarily a psychological rather than an educational concern.

Whatever their qualitative nature, emotions involve the utilization of large amounts of energy. An emotion can constitute a powerful source of gratification or create dysfunctional anxiety. A number of personality theories are based on the simple but valid premise that people do what they enjoy and avoid that which makes them feel anxious, i.e., they act to maximize pleasant emotions.

Most institutions, including education, tend to be suspicious of displays of either positive or negative emotion. Such displays are viewed as a distraction or a danger, because they lead people to do the unpredictable. This orientation is unfortunate. Emotions are not like an appendix, a regrettable hangover from a previous evolutionary era. They are the water of life. An existence without emotion is dull, dreary, gray, endless. It is the life of a robot. Because emotions are

23

among the most powerful motivators we have, utilizing their power in teaching vitalizes the enterprise. If a student enjoys what he is doing, the teacher has no real problem other than giving him enough material to keep him occupied. If the student is bored, if he feels nothing for the subject, and is negatively oriented toward the situation because of the way in which he is treated, it is difficult to teach him anything.

This does not mean that the student should do only what he wants to do in the classroom. This would be a perversion of the concept. Often it is precisely that which we do not want to do, that which we are afraid of doing, that must be done if we are to take a crucial step in maturation and understanding. Rather it implies that education must be concerned with emotions and that this concern must be primary. The emotions are there. If they are not developed and utilized for purposes of self-improvement and development they will recur in a destructive or distracting form. By ignoring and repressing them, educators may eliminate their most potent ally in the teaching process.

A striking contrast to the educator's approach to emotional expression is provided in dynamic psychotherapy, which assumes that the early socialization process conducted by family and peer groups has for some reason produced immature emotional patterns. Hence it is necessary to continue the emotional education of the individual through the use of specialized interpersonal situations such as counseling. Although there are a large number of psychotherapies, three contrasting procedures will be described to illustrate the range of possible approaches.

The first method, *Gestalt therapy,* has been developed over the last twenty years but has become widely known only recently.[2] The term *Gestalt* refers to the fact that we perceive in whole patterns. Gestalt therapy is designed to reintegrate the individual through expansion of his awareness of his inner experience and outer events. This is achieved by emphasizing the reality of the present. The individual is asked to report his experience as it happens. *I* might report this as follows:

I am hitting the typewriter keys. I hear the noise. My stomach rumbles. My neck is stiff. I can still taste the hot chocolate I just drank. My head is getting tight. My chest feels warm.

As this process continues, the individual will begin to go from the immediacy of the present into memories of the past or daydreams of the future. When this occurs, it is assumed that there is something about the present that the individual finds difficult to face. The therapist watches and waits for such signals and brings them into the awareness of the individual. The signals may involve not only avoiding the present but also performing contradictory behavior in the present. The therapist watches for signs of inconsistency between words and actions. For example, the person may be angrily describing some social injustice while his hands make vague and weak motions. Simply bringing the person's attention to this inconsistency may help to reintegrate his awareness. If this is insufficient, the therapist may resort to another basic technique in Gestalt therapy, "becoming that which is rejected." The person is asked to "become his hands and say what they are feeling." This is reasonable from the Gestalt point of view. Everything in the field of awareness is the individual. The field cannot be separated from the self. He influences the field and it influences him. This view has much in common with the field theory approach in physics, where instead of focusing on structure and particles, one visualizes interpenetrating fields of force. When the individual enacts the role of his hands, he gains more understanding of a part of his behavior of which he was unaware.

Another form which this reintegrative effort may take is the performance of the multiple roles that exist within the individual. One of the traditional dichotomies in Gestalt work is "top dog vs. underdog." The top dog is the authoritarian dogmatic principle in the individual telling him what to do, much like the super ego in psychoanalytic terms. The underdog is the weak individual cowering before the stronger parental figure. In Gestalt therapy the patient may take both parts alternately. By taking both roles he helps to reduce the distance between them.

The Gestalt orientation is most clearly seen when working with dreams. The dream is recreated as vividly as possible while the dreamer systematically enacts every person in the dream, saying what they said, expressing what they felt. He does this not only for the persons but for objects, such as walls, chairs, or stones. This extensive identification with varied elements helps him to understand the dream and assimilate its content. There is little or no effort to interpret the dream by the therapist. His function is, rather, to help the person relive and reexperience the content more completely than he could allow himself to do at the time when the dream occurred.

A second approach to emotional reeducation is *role construct therapy* developed by George Kelly.[3] In contrast to Gestalt therapy, Kelly's approach ignores the present and attempts artificially to create a new future. The first stage in role construct therapy is to diagnose the individual in a rather traditional manner. When his characteristics are identified, a new role is constructed that contains a number of characteristics that the individual does not possess. If he is quiet, the new person may be noisy. If he is curious, the new person may be indifferent. But the new role is not simply a list of characteristics. It is a person such as a playwright might create. Having developed the role on paper, the person is given the opportunity to rehearse it in various improvised situations. After thus gaining some confidence that he can in fact perform the role, the individual is encouraged to act the new person for a day or two, after which he returns to discuss the results. The basic principle behind this procedure is that most people are far more flexible than they realize. Given sufficient practice and encouragement, they can vary their behavior to a degree they might not have considered possible.

Role construct therapy constitutes an interesting and effective way to learn about one's own limitations and the ease with which certain kinds of change can be attained. Although the simple alteration of a behavior pattern cannot be equated with a personality change (as in hypnotism), nevertheless if a person can change his own patterns in normal situations, it must affect his self-image and give him a conscious possibility for future growth.

A third and contrasting method of emotional reeducation is *psychoanalysis,* an approach with which most persons are relatively familiar, if not by direct experience then through the mass media. Psychoanalysis resembles Gestalt therapy more closely than role construct therapy. It is relatively open-ended. The individual is asked to associate freely. He can go into the past or the future, or he can simply daydream. He is not limited to immediate sensations and impressions as in Gestalt therapy. The therapist will occasionally comment on the free associations and make interpretations of what they mean. A Gestalt therapist would do neither, being concerned only with extending awareness, not explaining it. Psychoanalysis is a verbal process. The individual is an observer of his own experience, and he reports it as directly as he dares. He does not act out different parts of his personality, and he does not try to create new roles that demand unfamiliar kinds of behaviors from him.

There are a large number of different psychotherapies currently in use, but the three discussed above are sufficient to illustrate the range of assumptions and methods that can be utilized. The reeducation of emotions has received much attention, although the integration of intellectually oriented education with emotional reeducation has been only slightly explored.

Applications

An important application of emotional reeducation is the improvement of motivation to learn by relating the learning process to positive emotional states. Many students feel they are incompetent in one or more subjects. If their emotional reactions to such failure could be countered, their performance might improve. This can be done by utilizing an approach developed by Paul Bindrim called peak-oriented psychotherapy.[4] A combination of relaxation, pleasant sensory experience, and visualization induce a positive emotional state in the individual. In a learning context this approach might be adopted as follows:

> I know that many of you think you are no good in this subject [mathematics, art, language]. Maybe you have had some bad experiences in the past. But you may have far greater ability than you realize. We tend to forget what we are capable of achieving, how long we can go without sleep, how quickly we can work when under pressure, how deeply we can feel under certain circumstances. Take a moment now and think over some of the high points of your life. Recall a time when you felt wonderful. When you were happy, inspired, free, when you did something you didn't think you had in you, something of which you are proud. . . .
>
> Now forget about that for the moment. I want you to relax as much as possible. Simply let the chair support you. Become aware of your breathing. Let your tension leave you as your breath leaves you. When you breathe in, feel new energy entering you, filling your whole organism.

After continuing these sorts of suggestions, proceed along the following line:

> Think of an odor that you love. Experience it as vividly as possible. Enjoy it. Bathe in it. Now think of a taste. Experience it as clearly as you can. Remember something you love to touch. Sense what that feels like. Hear a beautiful sound— music, wind, whatever you love. Finally, picture to yourself a beautiful scene.
>
> Now recall the incident you were thinking of before, the peak experience. Don't try to remember it. Just let it emerge. Try to sense any odors or sounds that may be occurring. Is the wind blowing? Do you see colors? Can you hear anyone speaking? How does your own body feel? Are you moving? Reexperience the situation as vividly as you can. I will be silent for a few minutes.
>
> Now open your eyes. There have been many such experiences in your life. You are capable of feeling, sensing, and thinking much more fully and deeply than you imagine. In a

moment we are going to return to the subject of this class. When we do, hold on to the mood that you have now. Even if you do not understand what I am saying at first, you will understand later. Hold the feeling. You have the power. It will work itself out as we go along.

A major use of cultivating emotional expression is to improve motivation for learning. For example, a teacher might walk into a restless room with a prepared lesson. He launches ahead, but the class is listless and disinterested. Joking and fighting start. Instead of disciplining the class, he might utilize the situation as an opportunity for some Gestalt "here and now" therapy as follows:

"I want you to tell me whatever you are experiencing right now. Just call it out. One after the other."

"I'm tired." "I see Harry's shirt." "I feel scared."

After some of these expressions have occurred, the teacher selects a student and works briefly with him.

"George, what is that in front of you?"

"A book."

"Be the book and say what it is thinking."

"Are you kidding?"

"No."

"Alright. Hey, stupid, aren't you going to read me?"

"Talk back to it."

"I don't like you. You are hard to read. You make me feel stupid."

"But if you don't read me, you really are going to be stupid."

"I don't care. It doesn't matter to me what I am or what you are."

"All right, be your brains inside your head and talk to the book."

"You make me feel silly. I look at you and feel like jelly. I don't like that. Why don't you talk so I can understand you? I want to learn things."

After some more of this kind of interaction, the teacher says:

"Now I am going to talk to my stomach. 'How are you, stomach?' 'I don't feel so good, I am tight. Those kids make me nervous. They don't like me. I have to defend myself against them.'"

Such an exchange requires no more than five or ten minutes. It could help to clear the air and enhance the students' readiness not only for the immediate lesson but for the rest of the day's activities.

Such interchanges depend on the experience of the teacher, his awareness of the immediate situation, and his skill in employing a variety of approaches. The teacher might reverse roles and ask the class to become the teacher while he acts as the difficult class. He might ask the students to draw pictures expressing how they were feeling. He might have a one-minute screaming session (assuming an understanding principal and good sound insulation). He might have the students write a five-minute essay titled, "Why I hate to study" or "Why I hate my teacher." He might have five minutes of "pay no attention to the teacher regardless of what he does," and then proceed to do anything that might gain the students' attention. There are numerous such cathartic methods.

A Class in Emotional Expression

Emotions are now admitted into classroom activities in two forms. Improvisation classes train actors to be able to express any required feeling. Encounter group training provides the expression of feelings as a prelude to learning more effective methods of handling emotional energy.

A student needs to be able to express convincingly any emotion just as he needs an adequate vocabulary. A variety of means is available to help generate feeling. He can recall situations from his own life when he had a particular feeling. He can create a character who would feel the given emotion. He can participate in acting, where it is permissible to feel in ways that might be irrelevant or highly inappropriate in everyday life. But when this is not enough, some corrective approach is necessary. A person must learn about his emotional patterns through letting them emerge in a group where they are clearly visible.

Emotional experiences can be described in terms of their variety, quality, and intensity. The cultivation of variety involves the kinds of exercises employed in acting classes, learning to experience any feeling at will, no matter how crude or refined. The focus of a particular session may be on just one feeling, such as jealousy, or continually shift from one to another in order to develop flexibility. Working with emotion in this way helps the person to diagnose and understand his own range and limitations. These limitations can often be extended through the more personal type of encounter work, in which the emphasis is not upon variety and subtlety of expression but on facing reality and challenging those aspects of emotion that the individual finds most threatening, often through a direct frontal attack.

In order to integrate these approaches some diagnostic system for measuring the individual's emotional expression is necessary. For example, such a system could be approximated by a standardized set of situations in which a large variety of different emotions would be expressed. The accuracy and intensity of these enactments could be rated by a group of judges, both as a basis of success in the course and more important to provide the individual with a profile of his functioning so that his work could be focused on his weakest areas. In summary, expressive methods for training actors used in conjunction with encounter group experience offer a varied and intense approach to the cultivation of emotions.

CHAPTER FIVE

VISUALIZATION AND IMAGINATION

VISUALIZATION is the ability to picture clearly a given object. Certain professions such as architecture and engineering depend heavily upon it. Imagination is a broader concept. A person with a vivid imagination can create an inner world of events. Most persons possess greater powers of imagination than they suspect. If hypnotized, they can hallucinate to a startling degree. For example, if a subject is told that an ash tray is red hot, he will cry out in pain if he touches it. He can be made to see things that are not there and not see things that are. This is not play-acting but a restructuring of perceptual experience along the lines suggested by the hypnotist.

The individual can relive scenes from his past, vividly and with an astonishing degree of recall. He can engage in fantasy with complete conviction. These are typical hypnotic phenomena. They simply require a certain relation between hypnotist and subject and a degree of direct suggestion. The individual does the rest.

Imagination is usually thought to be a negative quality, a distraction from realistic problem-solving activities. We ignore its existence, seek to suppress its more obvious manifestations, or accept it with reluctance as useful in artistic and literary enterprises if suitably controlled by appropriate technical skills.

· Imagination, like emotion, is a threat to the status quo. If people begin to explore other alternatives to the accepted social definition of reality, they may act in new and unpredictable ways or begin to question the efficacy of older ways. This makes us distrustful of such persons. We are not trained to welcome alternate possibilities but to be afraid of them.

Although the use of guided imagination for studying and altering the individual personality is in only the rudimentary stages of development, it nevertheless offers an extremely powerful means of harnessing unconscious creative forces. But for this to occur, imagination and visualization must be treated with respect and systematically trained not to fulfill a specialized requirement for a particular profession, but as a basic aspect of personal development.

The cultivation of visualization or imagination has generally been taken for granted as an individual ability or developed in conjunction with overall artistic performance. There have been few attempts to train visualization directly. One early approach is found in the work of C. H. Hinton.[1] The fundamental object employed in this system for the development of the powers of visualization is a multicolored cube. The student is led through a series of exercises of increasing difficulty, starting with one cube which is seen from different angles and leading through various patterns of cubes.

When the student has attained some degree of success, he is introduced to the motion of "self" elements and "object" elements in the visualization process. The self elements are those that the individual puts on the object. Thus, when we perceive the sun as turning around the earth, it is because of a self element that we impose on the situation. We know that the accurate perception is the earth circling the sun. Self elements are seductive because we do not suspect their existence until the moment we are made aware of them. We assume that we are seeing things as they are simply because we are accustomed to the given perception.

From the viewpoint of visualizing cubes, the self element is the angle of vision. A cube exists equally from every side at once and from the inside as much as the outside—it is only the limits of our perception that introduce an angle of vision. This limitation can be eliminated in the process of visualization. We can learn to see the cube from several directions at once, just as we can learn to play two different rhythms simultaneously. Thus visualization extends beyond perceptual reality and helps us to approach the object in itself, something that the senses themselves can never perceive. Hinton feels that such training has important intellectual implications. It provides a concrete approach to the understanding of objectivity and helps the individual to distinguish between his own subjective states and the reality on which they are imposed.

The study of imagination as distinct from visualization has generally come under the province of psychology. Much attention has been devoted to the interpretation of imaginative products, such as daydreams, night dreams, and artistic productions. But the imaginative faculty itself has been overlooked.

In the arts there is some effort to train imagination as a prelude to the creative process. This may take the form of theater games, creative writing exercises, or free painting. While such activities are valuable, they share the common property of preparing an individual to produce an external product. They are not designed to help him to understand or change himself through the use of guided imagination. The exception to this general situation is found in certain psychotherapies that employ guided imagery. A simple example of such an approach is the "who am I?" method of personal exploration by the Canadian psychologist, Martha Crampton. She begins by helping the individual to relax, because physical tension interferes with the visualization process. When the person is in a comfortable state, he is instructed as follows:

Close your eyes and imagine that you are surrounded by darkness. There is nothing to see. Let your eyes rest quietly.
Now imagine yourself somewhere in space, slowly approaching your own outermost layer . . . as if you were an artichoke or an onion. You are coming closer to the outer layer. In a moment you will reach it. Don't try to visualize anything in particular. Just tell me whatever you see. It may be an image, a scene, a person. What do you see?

(*The person responds. After he finishes, the instructions continue.*)

Now move on to the next layer. What do you see?

(*The person reports.*)

In a moment you are going deeper into yourself, to the third layer. . . .

The process usually continues through at least seven layers. Toward the end the instructions alter slightly.

You are almost at the center of yourself. This is the last layer before you reach it. What do you see?

(*He reports.*)

Now you are at the center of yourself. What do you see?

This simple repetitive procedure generally provides responses of great personal importance, surprising to both the subject and the listener. A person may feel that he is completely empty inside. He may begin with a pleasant scene, come to a place where things become ominous, and finally break through into an area of light, warmth, and happiness.

This procedure is an example of a guided daydream. It helps a person to interpret his inner state through the use of visual symbols that he generates for himself. Because the process was derived from a clinical context, the main purpose to which it has been put is self-understanding. In principle, there is no reason why the same approach could not be used to study any complex phenomenon the individual wanted to understand more fully, such as an atom or an interpersonal situation, each of which can be viewed as an event with layers of meaning.

An interesting extension of this approach that has been developed in encounter group work is the group dream. The dream is public so that one person's vision can affect another's. In one method people consciously try to build on each other's dreams. In another they have their own dream, while listening to those of others, being affected by them indirectly, if at all. A more limited version of a group fantasy is one in which two persons work out an interpersonal problem through shared fantasy. For example, if two persons are antagonistic to each other they may be instructed as follows:

Sit opposite one another. Close your eyes. Now imagine yourself as you are, across from one another. In a moment you are going to have a fight. When you start, I want you each to report out loud what is happening. Begin!

"I reach forward and push him over. He falls over like a wooden duck."

"As I go over, I kick out with my feet and hit him in the chest. His face turns white."

"I take a deep breath and throw myself forward. His legs get in my way but I pound him with my fists. I can't get to his face."

"I straighten out my legs, push him away and do a backwards somersault. Now I am on my feet."

"I am getting very angry. I rush at him. I want to see blood."

"I see him coming. I duck down at the last minute. He goes right past me and lands on the floor."

"Now I am really angry. I reach out and grab his leg and pull him down. As he comes down somehow my elbow hits him in the face. His nose starts to bleed. I really feel good."

The process continues until it comes to a resolution of some kind. One person wins the fight or they come to terms, for example. The value of this kind of fantasy is that it allows people to live through actions that might be socially destructive if acted out. After the aggression and anger have been expressed, it may be possible to lay the groundwork for a more constructive relationship. So long as the feeling remains suppressed, no real understanding or cooperation may be possible. Daydreaming in a group need not be limited to the expression of aggression. It can focus on any issue that is presenting difficulty between people—the expression of affection, distrust, or understanding. It can also be used as a means of creative problem solving without any strong emotional component.

Applications

A major use of imagination involves the enhancement of motivation for learning. It is difficult to maintain continuous interest in any subject if there is no reason to study it other than imposed necessity. Imagination can be used to help a person clarify in his own mind the uses to which given material may be put in the future and in this manner enhance his present motivation to persevere. For example:

> I want to stop this lecture for a moment and ask you to perform a task. I want you to daydream. I don't care whether it is farfetched or not. Close your eyes and see yourself in a situation in which what we have been studying would be important for you to know. Allow the situation to develop like a scene in a play. After a few minutes we can share experiences if you want to.

Another application of visualization and imagination relates them to the study of specific subject matter. The use of visualizing in the normal teaching process is relatively unexplored. With the exception of a few subjects that require visualization, such as drafting, solid geometry, and visual arts, the possibilities have been largely ignored.

Consider the following varied applications to English, physics or general class activities:

> We have just discussed the basic theme of *A Tale of Two Cities*. For the next few minutes I want you to shut your eyes and imagine as vividly as you can that part of the story which most clearly illustrates its general theme.

> I have just described what happens to water when an electric current passes through it. Shut your eyes and visualize yourself as very, very small. You are no bigger than the molecules and atoms. Experience what happens when an electric current is turned on. What do you see? What do you feel?

> Visualize in front of you a test of the material that I have just covered. Whenever you are ready, look at the questions one by one. Don't make them up. Just read them off and see whether you can answer them.

I have just finished presenting some material on primitive man. Do you think it could have been done better? Could you do it better? Shut your eyes and imagine yourself presenting the same material. Do it any way you wish. Go ahead.

In this manner imagination, which is usually a distraction, can become a powerful tool in the teaching process.

A Class in Imagination

Imagination is the capacity to redesign experience. It is a necessary but not sufficient condition in undertaking any behavior change. If we cannot visualize ourselves as different, the likelihood of ever changing is small.

If imagination has such potential importance, why is it put to so little use? Mainly because we do not know how to use it. Either we have never been trained or we use it more as an escape from reality than as an approach to redefining it. Perhaps one major reason we have been willing to ignore this powerful faculty is that we do not want the responsibility of using it. It is easier to drift in the current of events rather than attempt to influence them by visualizing how they might become.

How can a class in visualization and imagination be conducted? Hinton's approach to the cultivation of visualization is systematic and can be pursued as an independent activity or a smaller part of a study of the larger topic of imagination.

There are many interesting and significant things that we can take as the focus of imagination: how we look to other people, how we wish a past situation had turned out, our self as we would like to become, fantasies designed to tap the deeper levels of our functioning, the successful performance of a difficult task, another person in a better state, a group of people, a small society, people who are dead and those who have not been born, the actions of world leaders, the experiences of members of other cultures. All such situations are of potential interest. All may help the individual un-

derstand something about himself and the world as he views
it.

A variety of exercises intended for other purposes can
also be adapted to this end. For example, work on perceptual
awareness can be done in the imagination. We can be trained
to imagine a color or sound of a given quality and characteristic, and then test the accuracy of the experience by comparing it to the real stimulus.

In a more general sense the average person's social existence is too well defined to permit the individual either the
flexibility or the time to begin to experiment with the possibilities that are present at every moment. Nevertheless, the
fulfillment of human potential depends on a growing awareness of possibilities—some exciting, some frightening, some
funny, and others bewildering, some glorious, others disas-
trous, but all involved in the panorama of behavior. Imagination is the key to all this experience that we ordinarily lack
the time, energy, or courage to live out in reality. In a more
immediate sense imagination is the instrument through
which the individual can slowly fashion and control both his
own environment and his inner condition. Every function
can be approached through imagination. We can visualize
ourselves moving beautifully or seeing more fully or sensing
more deeply. Imagination is the power that the individual
has to guide his own growth. For this to be possible, imagination must be appreciated and trained.

CHAPTER SIX

EMPATHY

OUR intimate relations with others depend on our understanding of others. Although we may have difficulty in defining the form and content of this understanding, we do not doubt that it exists. Empathy is the term we use to describe our ability to put ourselves into the position of another.

Our more pedestrian experiences are based on role expectations. We have neither the need nor the motivation to look much beneath the surface in such situations. We do what is expected of us, and the other parties act in a way that we anticipate from them. But life is far more subtle than any system of role expectations can possibly predict. When expectations break down, empathy must take over or we find ourselves completely at a loss. If the other were truly a stranger, there could be no basis for a common understanding. To the extent that we see him as we see ourselves, we can discover both who he is and what we ought to do about him.

Social psychologists have devoted much attention to the study of empathy under a variety of different names, including social perception, interpersonal perception, social sensitivity, and empathy itself. They have focused on the' characteristics in the perceiver that are associated with empathic ability as well as the kinds of persons who are perceived most readily. Although the improvement of empathic ability has been largely ignored in these studies, a number of methods exist that can be employed for this purpose.

Perhaps the most direct approach is training the individual to act as a psychodramatic double. The function of the "double" is to become another version of an individual already in the psychodrama, usually the main character. The double is introduced when an individual cannot understand or describe aspects of himself. The double is an extension of the individual who can say and do things the individual might not feel free to express about himself. To double for anyone else, an individual must, of course, be able to empathize with him. The best way to train a double is through direct experience. For example, the double may imitate the posture of the individual being doubled. If you cross your legs while acting as a double, because the other person is doing so, you become aware of subtleties ordinarily overlooked through visual observation. You can sense how the legs feel. Are they comfortable or tense? What emotional state seems to go with that position?

The process is more indirect than that. The double is not only trying to understand what the person is experiencing but what he is not allowing himself to experience. Thus, if the person is expressing affection, the double may express anger, on the theory that the individual is not allowing himself to vent anger, even though deeper down he does feel it. At first the subject may protest if the double attributes such emotions to him. If the double is right in his understanding of the other, however, the other will shortly recognize it and act upon the anger within himself.

Doubling is a direct approach to the cultivation of empathy. As one goes through this process with persons of different backgrounds, ages, personalities, and motivations, one develops a facility in understanding and expressing the inner experiences of other individuals. Although some have a greater natural ability in this area of functioning than others, my experience in the training of psychodramatic personnel has shown that this kind of performance can be cultivated. In a broader sense most people think that understanding human nature is exclusively the province of experts and professionals. However, in group therapy and encounter groups, members may understand each other better than they would like. One exercise sometimes used to begin such experiences is to have each person stand in front of the group while other persons give their first impressions. Those who have gone through this exercise testify that it can be devastating in the clarity and the degree of insight shown by group members who are at that point strangers to one another. The problem, if there is one, is for participants to feel free to express what they really think and see. When they do, they may express observations about personal qualities that one would suppose would require extensive clinical study to detect.

Attempting to "read" a stranger can be used as a method of learning empathy when information about the individual is available from other sources. We could take from a novel a small extract involving a character and ask people to describe him, using the rest of the novel to confirm the degree of accuracy of the projection. There are many forms of this basic approach, each leading to the enhancement of the social sensitivity of the observer. In one study, for example, a movie was made of subjects during a stress interview.[1] Then extensive field studies were undertaken through conversations with friends, family, and acquaintances of the subjects to determine precisely how they acted in a variety of specific life situations, such as walking into a crowded room with a party in progress or coming home after a long day's work. Observers watching the movie of the original stress interview were asked to state how the individual would act in these other life situations about which objective evidence was available. This material was used as a means of measuring empathic ability. It could with equal facility be used to train empathy. A group of individuals observing the movie could evaluate the accuracy of their own predictions in order to learn more about the kinds of clues to look for and the nature of their own response biases. A related approach would be to employ anthropological materials. Observers watching movies taken in different cultures could be asked to interpret what was happening without knowledge of the culture involved.

Although this type of training may not be essential for a mature adult who relies on his understanding of roles to see him through most standard interpersonal situations, it is crucial for anyone who is interested in altering or developing the relationships in which he is involved. It is also useful for the child seeking to understand and interpret the mysterious ways of the adult. Task efficiency may require that we differentiate role performances, but communication demands that we also maintain our innate capacity to understand each other by entering the experience of another. If we do one without the other, the effect can only be alienation both from others and finally from ourselves.

Applications

When we speak of empathy, we usually visualize one person seeking to understand another, but there is no reason why two people such as teacher and student cannot simultaneously attempt to empathize with each other. In that case we have a role reversal.

When two people separated by age and status switch roles with each other, the social and emotional distance between them is reduced. This in itself can lead to increased mutual understanding. Many of the difficulties we create are produced through lack of awareness of others rather than conscious intent. If we were more aware of the other person in the situation, we would quickly realize where our misunderstandings lie; but it is necessary to take the time and make the effort for this kind of realization to occur.

A second major application of empathy to the educational process involves increasing the student's identification with the subject matter. A simple way to make subject matter more relevant is to enhance the student's personal involvement with it. This can be done through the exercise of empathy if we extend the process beyond the interpersonal situation to take in other forms of organic and inorganic experience.

The following approach might be employed in a chemistry class:

I am now going to demonstrate the effect of exposing raw potassium to air. As you know from your reading, pure potassium is supposed to burst into flame when in contact with oxygen. This is why we keep it covered with fluid in this bottle. In a moment I will reach in with the tweezers, take out a piece, and place it on this asbestos mat. Before I do, I want you to identify with the potassium in the bottle. How does it feel? What does it think? Anyone who wishes, express what you sense out loud.

"It feels cold."
"It feels scared."
"It doesn't want to burn up."
"Yes, it does."
"It feels very powerful. It chuckles to itself."
"It wants to feel the oxygen and go up in flames."

Keep up what you are doing while I reach down in the bottle and take a small nugget of potassium out and put it on the table.

In an English class the following exchange might occur:

I am going to write a sentence on the board. Instead of simply analyzing each part of the sentence grammatically, I want you to try to become the sentence and see what it feels like. This is the sentence. "Everyone that was with us said nothing." How does that sentence feel to you? What would you be thinking if you were that sentence written up on the blackboard?

"I'd feel ashamed."
"I wish someone would erase me."
"I only like 'was with us.' The rest doesn't belong to me."
"I am not a sentence. I just look like a sentence."
"Take me down."

Now what precisely is wrong with that sentence grammatically?

In an art class the following approach might be employed:

I am showing on the screen a photograph of *Guernica*, a modern painting by the famous modern artist Pablo Picasso. Now for the moment I am not worried about why Picasso painted this picture, what technique he used, or even whether or not you like it. I only want you to experience more fully what it represents. Suppose that instead of sitting in your chairs you were in the picture. How would you feel? I don't mean that your whole body would be in the picture but that you would sense how the picture feels, what it thinks about. Try that a little bit. Write down what you experience. Then after a minute I am going to ask you to express out loud what you sense in the picture. (a minute elapses) Now out loud. . . .

"I just want to explode."

"I feel awful, bloody, wounded. This is a terrible place to be, but I can't get out."

"Everything is coming apart. Everything is detached. I will never get back together again."

"Who did this to me?"

"There are guns roaring all around and the smell of burning flesh."

"It is like music—barbaric, loud, horrible music. It keeps getting louder and louder."

Now let these impressions go and I'll tell you something about how and why this picture was created.

In all of these examples the same principle is employed. The student empathizes with the subject matter in order to enhance his involvement with it and to understand the mood underlying its existence or creation. When empathizing with a nonhuman phenomenon, we cannot directly check on the correctness of our observations. We cannot ask a chemical or a sentence whether it really feels that way, but this is relatively unimportant. What is significant is that the individual focuses his experience on the subject at hand and puts himself into a condition in which he will be more interested and receptive to the material to be discussed.

A Class in Empathy

In the study of empathy students are natural subjects for each other using the methods described such as doubling, role reversal and identifying. As they gain some sense of how to go about empathizing, they will become aware that they have blindspots for certain classes of people. Thus, they may discover that for members of the opposite sex, or of a different race they possess stereotypes which interfere with sensing the other person's actual state. Such discoveries are limits to personal growth.

As the opportunities in the classroom are exhausted, one can send teams to observe situations in the school or nearby community. The purpose of these visits is to select a given individual and attempt to empathize with him. The team members then compare notes and analyze disagreements that may exist in their conclusions. There are many other possibilities. Students may be sent out in two-person teams to visit one another's homes. The one member attempts to empathize with the other as they move through typical family situations. Students can be sent out on their own to observe a certain number of people in assigned situations such as a grocery store, a bank, a movie. Their observations can be kept in a notebook with particular attention devoted to describing any methods that were devised to help foster the empathic process. These notes are then brought back to class to be the basis for group discussion. Another approach is to use pictures and portraits of persons unknown to the student but about whom information is available. What can the students pick up about these people from observing their pictures?

One can become facile in reading other people. This is essentially an intellectual process, useful but insufficient. We must also develop sufficient depth so that we can feel the other as well as know him. Only from such an understanding can a bond of sympathy be generated and the action between the two persons be redefined. The empathy class is intended to cultivate both levels of human experience.

CHAPTER SEVEN

PARANORMAL ABILITIES

E VERY culture, including our own, records instances of paranormal abilities—telepathy, precognition, psychokinesis, clairvoyance. These instances of the unexplained and the misunderstood must represent something real in human nature even though science has not succeeded in clarifying the issues that are involved.

The history of research on paranormal phenomena in this century is strewn with bias, misconceived methodology, unrepeatable results, and occasional runs of remarkable data. The results have not convinced most behavioral scientists that paranormal abilities do exist, but few resources have been applied to the task. Researchers interested in psychic phenomena have often been ridiculed. Few psychologists have entered the field. Other scientists and interested amateurs who have pursued paranormal studies have usually done so as a side interest.

Nevertheless, faith in the existence of these phenomena is widespread. We either believe we have experienced or heard from others who have experienced events of a paranormal character—family members who appeared over long distances at the moment of death, dreams of the future, interlocking coincidences.

While only a decade ago the climate of opinion was skeptical, today it is inclined toward belief in a variety of occult, bizarre, and supernatural occurrences. For our purposes it is sufficient to have an open mind.

In one sense paranormal phenomena are extensions of normal ones, such as visualization, empathy, and creativity. It is possible that methods designed to improve those functions may inadvertently lead into the paranormal. There is, for example, a fine line between being highly empathic and possessing telepathic ability.

One difficulty that surrounds the development of psychic abilities is that the subject is generally cloaked in secrecy. As with any occult matter, the practitioners, if they are sincere, are reticent about their methods or simply possess natural gifts that they cannot transmit. There is also a strong possibility that some practitioners are faking, sometimes out of a desire to create a greater impression, sometimes because that is all they can do.

But just as chemistry grew out of alchemy and astronomy out of astrology, so out of paranormal experiences and inexplicable events may come a clear and reliable set of facts about forces in human nature that we have not recognized and do not cultivate. It is suggestive that in describing the education of the future, many science fiction writers have focused on schools for telepaths. Since science fiction has often been the outlet for creative minds who in a more professional capacity would limit their originality, something may exist behind this convergence of interest, even if it is only a common fantasy, such as the ability to fly without wings.

Many paranormal phenomena exist in our dreams and seem perfectly reasonable at the time. On waking we view them as fantasies. Paranormal phenomena may be waking fantasies. On the other hand such dreams may represent latent human functions, just as they symbolize inner human states. Before Freud, the notion of dreams as messengers of the unconscious was ridiculed. Today, dreams as symbols of human attainment may also be ridiculed as childish wish fulfillment. In the next century they may be revealed as half-disguised messages of our latent paranormal powers.

Most methods of developing psychic abilities are taught by personal instruction or are described in writing in a puzzling or misleading manner. One exception is a little book by Ophiel called *The Art and Practice of Astral Projection.*[1] Although the book has complexities, the instructions presented are simple.

Astral projection involves "leaving" the body while remaining fully conscious. Ophiel presents four methods for attaining this paranormal experience. These are the *little method,* the *dream method,* the *body of light method,* and the *symbol method.* Each of these will be briefly described to illustrate his approach.

The little method involves a combination of observation, visualization, and projection. The first step in the process is for the student to pick a definite route that he is going to take in his projection. After doing this he actually walks along this route, noting in detail every aspect of it. After this has been done many times, he selects a number of fixed points along the path to which he pays particular attention. A variety of sensations can be associated with these locations. Different scents may be placed by the student at these fixed points in order to make them more vivid in the memory.

The actual projection requires that the student relax in either a sitting or reclining position. Then he recalls the first fixed spot, realizing that this memory is also a projection. Each spot is recalled in the order in which it occurs in reality. When the end of the path is reached, the student returns, following the same sequence of steps as if climbing down a ladder.

When this process has become familiar, the student visualizes himself getting up and walking the path. He is then in two places at once, following the path in his imagination and lying or sitting in physical reality. His effort is to place his consciousness in the imaginary body. After a period of effort, it is said, he will begin to have the experience of being within the new body while still maintaining an awareness of the old. This is an outline of the little method of astral projection.

The dream method begins with a study of normal dreams. From this investigation the student learns that anything can appear natural in a dream, regardless of how strange or impossible it might seem when he is awake. The next point of concentration is to become more conscious while dreaming, or to attempt to avoid waking up when one has dreamed, so that the dream can continue with greater awareness on the individual's part. If there is sufficient desire and patience, a splitting of consciousness in the dream will eventually occur according to Ophiel. The dream will continue, but the individual will observe it as it occurs. The individual will be in two places at once, which is the basic aim of astral projection.

The body of light method consists in part of a mystical ritual that is not important for our purposes. The other aspects of this approach can be more simply described. A preliminary exercise is to view the right hand and examine it as if you were looking at it for the first time. Then move each finger as you say the name of the finger, from thumb to little finger and then back to thumb. This kind of exercise is repeated with growing frequency and then extended to other parts of the body. Each action is accompanied by the appropriate name. Practice is essential. At a certain point the individual visualizes with his eyes closed what is happening as he does it. Thus, he says the word, performs the action, and at the same time visualizes the action being performed.

After about six months of such practice the student should be able to visualize a body that moves as he moves. The rest of the work growing out of this method involves the ritual previously mentioned. The purpose is to give this visualized body vitality and flexibility so that it can be sent where the individual wishes it to go and do what he wishes it to do. The body of light is a second self, nonphysical and under control of the individual who created it.

The symbol method does not lend itself easily to brief description. The student makes a set of symbols of specified shapes and colors, each of which has a definite cosmological significance. Through a process of concentrated gazing at each symbol, the student learns how to enter the realm it represents. Special sounds and names are associated with each symbol and are designed to intensify and alter the particular experience each is said to contain.

The most striking aspect of all these methods is that they are essentially simple, but require constant repetition, careful preparation, and motivation. In themselves they are not terribly interesting, though their description is often clothed in mystical ideas and strange experiences.

The little method is based on sensory awareness and perceptual accuracy. The dream method involves an alternation of consciousness similar to certain forms of meditation. The body of light method is a visualization exercise utilizing physical motion as a means of heightening the imagery. The symbol method combines visualization, creativity, and the sounding of sacred names as in a prayer or mantra. All these approaches represent an extension or application of those already described elsewhere under the heading of other functions. In a sense this is reassuring. It suggests that paranormal abilities do not require unique human functions to manifest themselves. It also suggests that since the development of these other facilities seems to be possible, the experience of astral travel may also be subject to cultivation. This, of course, leaves open the question of how the experience is to be interpreted. Is it imaginary as a dream or does it constitute a real waking experience, unusual but not pathological? Only further study can clarify this issue.

Applications

It is difficult to attempt to apply methods designed to train faculties that may not exist or that seem to overlap with others dealt with elsewhere. However, one example can be cited for purposes of illustration. This involves solving a difficult problem, such as a mathematical exercise, by approaching it as an experiment in clairvoyance. For example:

From what a number of you have said, you really don't have the foggiest idea what to do with the eighth problem. For the moment I am not going to try to explain anything. But let us assume that somewhere, in a great mind, there is a solution of this problem. It is not in your mind, but it is in this other mind. If only you could locate that other mind and seek out its knowledge. But you don't know where to look. So here you sit, ignorant and frustrated.

Let's try an experiment. Settle back in your chairs, shut your eyes, and relax. Just sense a great, vast darkness around you. The more you relax, the darker it will become. Let the darkness invade you so that you and it are together and you extend as far as it goes, out into endless space.

Somewhere way out there, beyond your sight, is that other mind that contains the knowledge you need. Can you sense it? Perhaps it is a point of light. Perhaps only an invisible presence. Allow it to come closer to you. Flow in the darkness. Let the space between you be the bond that ties you together. Sense that mind. Feel the radiations it gives off. Allow them to reach you. It knows what you are thinking. It knows what you want. Let its thoughts come into your mind. Make no particular effort. Let the thoughts come like sunshine on a clear day. Let them lighten your ignorance. Can you sense a change in your inner state? Does something in you begin to understand? Don't force it. The knowledge is there like a newly planted seed. Be gentle with it. Give it a chance to grow.

Now slowly let the darkness recede and return into your own body and your own mind. Then, when you are ready, open your eyes and we will resume our studies.

The purpose of this exercise is not to prove anything about the existence of paranormal phenomena. It should, however, put the students into a state in which a deeper and more subtle contact is made with the subject matter under discussion.

A Class in Paranormal Abilities

A useful way to institute a class in paranormal phenomena is to share experiences in this area that students have already had or that their friends have described to them. This can be extended to reading case studies of such experiences. In addition students can record and analyze daily paranormal experiences that they have, and usually forget. Any such experience can be discounted as coincidence, but the purpose here is not to validate but rather to become more sensitive to the functioning of certain capacities that are recognized in other cultures but ignored or ridiculed in our own.

The work on astral projection of Ophiel described previously is straightforward. It requires continuous practice such as might be conducted in the classroom with students sharing their experiences with each other at each stage of the process.

A simple approach to the study and development of telepathic ability is the use of the symbol cards developed at Duke University by J. B. Rhine.[2] These cards contain one of five signs that the student is asked to guess before seeing the card. He has one chance in five of being correct. There are several ways in which the process can be varied. If he guesses the cards without looking at them, then clairvoyance is possible. If another person looks at the card before the guess is made, telepathy is possible.

Another approach is to place unknown objects out of sight and have students attempt to guess their nature. Students may be blindfolded and asked to tell something of the history of an object put in their hands. They can be asked to foretell one another's future.

Particular emphasis might be placed at each class meeting on the repetition of a set of tests designed to assess telepathy, clairvoyance, and other paranormal phenomena. Observations of success or failure and discussion of the process should help class members to develop new methods and learn from one another's failures.

Each of the activities is intrinsically interesting and can be viewed as diagnostic. If any genuine ability exists, it may come to light. It also helps students to get some sense of the process involved.

Another possible activity would be to have a reputable medium demonstrate how psychic ability functions in a person of unusual talents. Outside experts would, of course, be helpful in any of the classes, but it would be particularly helpful in a controversial area.

A further approach is to replicate famous experiments in paranormal psychology such as those summarized by Pratt *et al.* in *Extra-Sensory Perception After Sixty Years.*[3]

It would be particularly helpful to experiment with the effects that other human activities have on paranormal ability. It is not unlikely that sensory awareness, visualization, empathy, and other functions might facilitate the more subtle psychic abilities. This would provide an opportunity to examine the effect of different human functions on each other.

CHAPTER EIGHT

CREATIVE EXPRESSION

T HE swift pace of social change requires that we be able to solve problems that may not have existed when we were formally educated. Narrow specialization may leave us swamped by the tide of progress. Most traditional education does little to foster creative expression.

Creativity is recognized and approved in certain areas, particularly the arts, as essential for professional competence. But the purpose of artistic training, however valuable in itself, is not the enhancement of the individual experience but the development of an interesting product for which the individual is responsible, whether it be a book, a picture, or a stage performance. If the individual learns or is influenced by the creative process, it is incidental.

But what of the vast range of us who cannot put our originality into a professionally acceptable form? Are we to be shut off from the process of search and discovery? Is it irrelevant for our experience? Education seems to be based on such a premise. We go to school to be taught what is known. We do not discover, we assimilate. In spite of notable exceptions to this orientation, the overall trend is unmistakable—education is directed at the cultivation of the intellect. It emphasizes the presentation, digestion, and analysis of prepared materials; it emphasizes accuracy, not a range of responses.

Such an emphasis would be suitable if creativity and intelligence were part of some general ability such as adaptability to the environment. However, many studies that compare creativity and intelligence show that they are not.[1] In some respects they are antithetical. For example, the development of intellectual abilities must emphasize the learning and analysis of specific facts conforming to the laws of logic. The cultivation of creativity demands the temporary suspension of laws of logic with an emphasis on what might be called the laws of possibility. Most methods of creativity training specifically require the suspension of critical judgment in the earlier stages of the process, an act that would not be tolerated in the cultivation of intellect. The philosophy of academic testing is oriented toward logical intellectual procedures. If we suspend judgment, the notion of testing is partially irrelevant.

To the extent that education discourages creative expression, it reduces or eliminates that which we possessed as a child—the capacity to play, make believe, or try possible alternates in a half-real world. This is a loss, not only to the individual, but to society, which depends on innovation for survival.

Perhaps society cannot tolerate too much creativity and therefore does not encourage its development. Many social institutions expect little innovation from their members. They maintain a stable equilibrium and depend on faithful performance of specified roles. If a substantial number of the members of the institution begin to question whether the old way is necessarily the best, the equilibrium might be disturbed. Such questioning need not be destructive except when it is the consequence of accumulated grievances.

Unless the healthy organization or institution seeks to foster creativity it will tend to stagnate. Nothing that is alive can remain static. It must improve or decay. It may seem to survive without change, but it usually becomes a hollow shell of its original intent.

One of the most direct ways for enhancing creativity is to act as if we are creative. This orientation is most clearly developed in the description of the "creative subself," which involves an application of role playing to the development of creative expression.[2] The basic premise is that in each individual is the capacity to enact many roles. It should therefore be possible to identify and cultivate a "creative" role that can be assumed when necessary. Toward this end an individual can cultivate a subself with a specific personality of its own.

Thus "Mr. Lightloose" can become the personification of the more daring creative aspects of a more pedestrian Mr. Smith. Through fantasy and group discussion Mr. Lightloose can be encouraged. Then, when needed or desired, Mr. Smith permits Mr. Lightloose to emerge and allows him to function as completely and intensely as possible. When the need for creativity is diminished, Mr. Lightloose can depart and other more pedestrian subselves in Mr. Smith's repertoire can again gain the ascendancy.

A more elaborate approach to creative problem solving has been evolved during the past twenty years by a group working at the State University College at Buffalo under the direction of Dr. Sidney Parnes. The Creative Education Foundation they have established acts as a center for distributing information on recent research on creativity. It has also been active in developing and evaluating a specialized workshop approach to the cultivation of creativity. Several workbooks have been prepared as adjuncts to such training and are available for general use.[3]

Their basic approach combines a scientific problem-solving orientation with provision for brainstorming and other procedures designed to foster creative experiences. Perhaps the greatest single value of this approach is its degree of systematization. A typical problem-solving sequence would proceed through the following steps.

1. Identifying the "mess," i.e., problem for which the solution is sought.
2. Collecting relevant facts.

3. Raising relevant questions to which answers should be found.
4. Phrasing a preliminary statement of the problem.
5. Making a broader statement of the problem.
6. Identifying subproblems related to the overall problem and selecting the particular problem or subproblem on which to focus.
7. Listing every possible solution, noting those that seem unusual or strange.
8. Attempting to make strange solutions practical.
9. Determining the practicality of proposed solutions.
10. Evaluating solutions after they have been applied.

A more complex and subtle approach to the enhancement of creativity is Synectics.[4] This method combines group dynamics, problem solving, and creative brainstorming in a unique amalgam. Its major application has been in the area of industrial inventions, but the approach can apply to a variety of different problem areas including education.

The most striking single feature of the Synectics approach is that it involves the maintenance of a permanent problem-solving group that may function together for years. A second important feature is its reliance on a number of different forms of analogy to foster the creative process. This approach was developed slowly from an analysis of creative behavior and the various stages through which it could be observed to pass. The originators became convinced that no amount of descriptive or clinical study would tell them just what to do in order to enhance creativity. It was then that they hit upon the use of analogies as a means of improving the qualitative level of creativity within a group context.

Four types of analogies were distinguished:

1. Direct analogy: looking for a similar instance from another field of activity.
2. Symbolic analogy: looking for a poetic solution that might not be technically feasible.
3. Fantasy analogy: similar to free association. No reasonable thread need be maintained between the problem and the solution.

4. Becoming the object: taking the role of some part of the problem.

These techniques are employed in the Synectics group under the guidance of a leader who provides the group with information about the problem to be solved. Typically he describes it first only in the most general terms in order to avoid any tendency to settle prematurely on a solution. Only after much work does he reveal the precise nature of the problem. An hypothetical illustration may help to clarify how these analogies are employed in practice. The type of analogy used is indicated in parentheses.

LEADER: The general problem is in the area of relating.

"Relating is like 'talking to' or 'talking with.' " (symbolic analogy)
"When I relate I feel happy."
"Who am I relating to? That makes a big difference. There are a lot of things I don't want to have anything to do with."
"Relating is opening a door after someone has knocked. It is an oyster being pried open." (direct analogy)
"A monkey relates to a snake. He is too scared to move." (direct analogy)
"A bank teller relates to a robber. He is too scared to refuse."
"We relate to avoid trouble or because we will enjoy the process."

LEADER: Two different kinds of thing wish to relate differently to each other.

"First one and then the other."
"How about a man and a woman?" (direct analogy)
"What do you mean?"
"They relate differently to each other in sex."
"But what if they both want to have their backs to each other."
"They could use mirrors."
"A round peg in a square hole. How can you solve that?" (symbolic analogy)
"Make the hole large enough so that the square just fits."
"Make the square hole out of elastic so that it can be changed into a round shape without any space left over."
"What are we dealing with, animals, objects or people?"

LEADER: People.

"Making people flexible is like kneading dough." (direct analogy)
"What if one wants to be flexible and the other doesn't?"
"They could reverse roles."
"How would that help?"
"It would change their perspective. Let's try it. You be Mr. Round Hole. You want me to be flexible. I am Mr. Square Hole. I want to keep my shape."
"This isn't reversing roles."
"I know. Let's do it anyway." (Becoming the object.)
"O.K. square. Why are you so up tight? Don't you know round is a better shape?
"I know what's right. You don't. Stop trying to drag me down to your level with seductive logic."
"Boy, you really are something else."
"And stop using those stupid phrases. Next thing you'll be saying that I need to hang loose."
"I'm glad you realize it. Why don't you try to get into my head? Then maybe we could talk."
"You don't seem to have any respect for my experience. You just want everything to be reduced to your level."

LEADER: The problem concerns students and teachers.

"The relation between students and teachers? What part of the relation?"

LEADER: Free associate to students and teachers.

"Birds and worms . . . sun and moon . . . mother and child." (fantasy analogy)
"Power and slavery . . . computers and big eyes."
"Communicating . . . one way . . . two way . . . which way?"

LEADER: Students are complaining that teachers do not respect them as human beings.
"What's the problem?"

LEADER: The teachers disagree. They say they are not there to socialize, but to teach.

"What we have here is a failure to communicate."

LEADER: Before we go further I am going to play back a tape of our conversation up to this point to see what ideas it generates. . . .

This represents the first stage of a Synectics approach to solving the problem that has just been revealed. It combines group interaction with brainstorming, fantasy, and role playing under the guidance of a leader who helps the group to converge upon the problem while laying the groundwork for deriving a solution from the web of associations that has been generated in the process.

Applications

Both the creative problem-solving approach and the Synectics analogies lend themselves directly to the educational process, of which they are extensions. Each is designed to generate creative and effective solutions to problems an educator or a student might face. Consider the following examples:

1. A student is doing poorly in his work.
2. Activists are disrupting classroom activity.
3. Teachers are unwilling to use any but routine teaching methods.
4. Parents are concerned that students are not learning fundamental skills because of time spent in educational experimentation.
5. Students want to eliminate marks.

These kinds of situations can occur in any school. How would a creative problem-solving approach be used to deal with them?

The first step is to identify the mess. In problem 2 the mess involves the disruption of class activities by political activists who demand attention, use foul language, and are generally disruptive. What are the relevant facts? Which classes are disrupted? Who are the disruptors? What do they seek to accomplish? What do they accomplish? And so on.

What additional information is required? Are they part of some more general movement? Is a particular class or teacher their target? What is the attitude of the principal and the parents?

Restatement of the problem: How do you conduct a class when a small minority is bent on disrupting it? Broader statement of the problem: How can the rights of the majority be protected while preserving the rights of the minority? Related subproblems: Does the class support and or tolerate the dissenters? What is the teacher's own attitude? Does he sympathize? Does he feel that the disruptors are an affront to his authority? How are the disturbances instituted? How are they perpetuated? How are they ended? Is the leadership centralized or distributed?

After considering the foregoing it might be decided that the fundamental problem is maintaining a classroom atmosphere in which learning remains possible even under difficult conditions. This issue then becomes the focus of brainstorming, which might produce the following kinds of solutions:

1. Call the police at the first sign of disturbance.
2. Flunk students causing classroom disturbance.
3. Send the agitators to the mental health clinic for observation.
4. Stop all activity the instant a classroom disturbance begins. Do nothing until it ends.
5. Have the whole class scream back at the agitators.
6. Have the students attack the agitators.
7. Let the teacher mirror the agitators' behavior.
8. Use the disturbances as the basis of a discussion of democratic institutions.
9. Have the whole class make funny faces at the agitators.

Analysis of these alternatives suggest certain patterns. Alternatives 1, 2, 3, and 6 are punitive. Alternatives 4, 5, 7, and 9 are shocking. Only alternative 8 actually attempts to use the disturbance as an educational activity in its own right. The strangest solutions are probably 5 and 9, having the whole class scream back or having the whole class make funny faces at the agitators.

In evaluating the practicality of solutions 5 and 9 some of the following factors need to be considered. First, would the students seriously perform these tasks? Second, would these solutions exaggerate the problem or resolve it? Would having the students scream back at the agitators lead to a general riot or would the one group overcome the other? In contrast, would silent funny faces reduce the risk of contagion and form a kind of nonviolent protest that might verge into humor? It might prove hard for agitators to be disruptive if everyone turned around to watch them and made funny faces.

On the basis of this kind of analysis it is decided to use alternative 9. The class then practices the procedure using role playing to simulate the actual conditions. Finally, a real incident occurs, and it is possible to evaluate the success of the approach. Perhaps a deathly silence ensues when the agitator realizes what is happening. He then tries harder to be disturbing. After a few minutes he leaves in disgust and the class gets back to work after some joking and self-congratulation on the effectiveness of the strategy. The students then describe the incident in writing so that it can be compared to others of the same type employing the same or other solutions.

A Class in Creativity

Classes in the development of creative problem-solving ability, some in workshops, others organized as traditional courses, now exist. The Creativity Foundation at the State University College, Buffalo, New York, has developed a relatively elaborate set of materials for such a course. An arts approach to working with various creative media such as paints, clay, words, and photographs offers a variety of possibilities. The product is different from that developed by the Buffalo course, where the emphasis is on problem-solving. In contrast, artistic productions are intended to give pleasure, excitement, and beauty. Yet whether one creates in one's life or in a particular medium, the need to redefine reality in a new synthesis of conflicting and diverse elements remains a constant challenge.

It is hard to overemphasize the importance of the cultivation of creativity. Creativity is one of our most precious resources. It is a source of individual vitality and institutional strength.

Whether one emphasizes the nonjudgmental use of creative media or the application of creative problem-solving to professional and personal problems there is little difficulty in imagining a course on creativity. Three major approaches would be more than sufficient—techniques for the arts designed to enhance awareness and facility in the use of various media and materials; training in problem-solving through the use of an orderly integration of logic with creative emphasis on unexpected solutions; a Synectics approach combining small group functioning with creative breakthroughs by the use of analogies. Each of these experiences contains more than enough material for a single course. Together they should constitute a powerful combination for awakening the individual to his own creative resources.

CHAPTER NINE

INTELLIGENCE

MOST education is so top-heavy in its emphasis on intellectual pursuits that we inevitably assume the intellect to be systematically cultivated at the expense of almost everything else. Although much student time is devoted to learning facts and assimilating ideas, this is not the same as cultivating the mind, even though the successful student does learn something of how to think more efficiently as he goes along.

Just as most people read much more slowly than they might, so possibly students learn much more inefficiently than is necessary. How many students ever take a course in how to study? Such courses are usually reserved for those in academic difficulty, just as reading courses are given for poor readers. I see no reason for this lack of training. In spite of the numerous books and outlines on how to study available, they are not employed in the classroom on a wide scale. They might be used in a class on intellectual development. Granted the materials available vary widely in quality and would have to be chosen with care.

A rather different approach would be to cultivate the various facets of intellectual performance that have been identified through extensive factor analytic investigation of the dimensions of intelligence. Perhaps the best known of these approaches is the model of the "structure of intellect" developed by Guilford, which suggests 120 intellectual abilities.[1] Although the specific elements in the model are subject to modification, its basic usefulness is that it not only divides intellect into independent categories but also indicates ways of testing for each category. Using this scheme or a simplified version of it, it is possible to diagnose the level of individual achievement in each area, not in our case for purposes of obtaining an overall measure but rather as the basis for further training to correct diagnosed weaknesses.

Guilford distinguishes three categories, each of which enters into any given measurement of intellectual functioning. These are operations, contents, and products. A given ability utilizes a particular operation on a given content producing a definite product.

There are five major operations: cognition or the recognition of relationships, memory, convergent thinking or logical problem solving, divergent thinking or the forming of unusual associations, and evaluation.

There are four types of contents toward which the operations are directed: figural, such as photographs; symbolic, such as letters and numbers; semantic, involving patterns of symbolic meanings; and behavioral, concerning the observation of social action.

The products that result from the application of operations to contents are divided into six categories: units, such as a specific object; classes that are an organization of units; relations between different classes; systems that involve a pattern among relationships; transformations, concerning changes in the meaning of units; and implications, involving the ability to foresee conclusions that go beyond the information available.

Any given intellectual ability consists of a particular content joined with a given operation producing a given product. For example, the factor that Guilford calls "configuration" describes the cognition of figural material arranged as unit products. This factor is involved in the perception of incompleted pictures that are formed through cognition into complete forms. The picture is figural and the completed figure is a unit. In Guilford's model there are 119 other unique combinations of operations, contents, and products, most of which have been associated with existing tests of intellectual performance. The diagnostic possibilities are vast and the training avenues equally diverse.

The average curriculum is not concerned with the various aspects of intelligence, as such. Certain facets, such as memory and convergent thinking, may be highly developed and others ignored. This is not a conscious choice but rather an indirect effect of the kinds of materials believed to be essential for each area of specialization. The intellectually developed individual should be able to function with all kinds of operations, contents and products, a possibility that could be approached in a class devoted to the cultivation of the many aspects of intelligence.

CHAPTER TEN

ETHICAL VALUES

A vital complement to the development of inner experience is ethical functioning. One can take two views in regard to ethics. The first is that it is an inheritance from the past to be taught to and absorbed by the young. This view need not concern us here because it does not involve individual growth and development so much as the inculcation of a strong super ego, preferably outside of the individual's control so that he cannot tamper with it.

A second approach is that ethics consists of a set of empirically derived guides or principles that the individual develops in the process of maturing. These principles may overlap or even be identical with those widely spread throughout society or they may contradict or deviate from them. Nevertheless they represent the crystallization of the individual's life experience, rather than a set of principles given to him by some representative of society.

We often assume that most people must be made to do what is good for them, but for the individual devoted to learning about himself and his functioning no absolute principle coming from some unquestionable source is acceptable. He must at least have the possibility of testing it.

In simplest form our ethics define what is right and what

is wrong. Contemporary thought holds also that ethical principles are highly relativistic. Right in one society may be partially wrong in another; right for an individual in one situation may be wrong in another. We are all taught not to lie, yet there are situations in which we may be severely penalized if we tell the truth. Our society is riddled with such internal contradictions.

The teaching of ethics is generally considered to be old-fashioned, perhaps because it has been undertaken in a routine and unimaginative manner. Some efforts in this area are more sophisticated, utilizing modern pedagogy, a scientific orientation, and an enlightened view of what character education might involve. Although their impact has not been great, their existence is encouraging. Three illustrations can be cited.

The first is described by Virginia Trevitt in her book *The American Heritage—Design for National Character*.[1] Through lecture, discussion, and personal experimentation students are encouraged to apply the ideals of the founding fathers to their own lives. This program utilizes the obvious but unappreciated fact that many of the principles to which the United States was dedicated are well suited to the needs and ideals of today's youth. The emphasis on rebellion, autonomy, the protection of minorities, the right to happiness, and a return to religious experience in contrast to formalistic observance is timely. Principles that might have seemed outdated ten years ago have taken on a new timeliness today.

A second example is a project in value education that was conducted by the San Francisco YMCA's over a five-year period.[2] At the heart of the effort was an attempt to redefine ethical values and a willingness to employ innovative methods in order to achieve a more effective program of value education.

Extensive use was made of the small group situation as the agent of change. Materials were prepared to guide staff in the formation and leadership of groups. Various topics and other program aids were devised and perfected, as well as evaluation tools. The project constituted an interesting case study of institutional change in a setting in which ethical values were of prime concern.

Perhaps the most interesting attempt to integrate religious principles with scientific methodology is the Character Research Project conducted by Dr. Ernest Ligon over the last three decades.[3] This project constitutes one of the most lengthy programs of research in the social sciences. Its essential purpose has been to develop materials for teaching Christian principles of conduct utilizing modern scientific and pedagogical methods. Although some of the materials that have been developed by Dr. Ligon and his associates lend themselves to school use, he has devoted particular attention to approaches that could be applied within the family setting. The materials themselves are complex, relying on both standardized printed matter and a continuous interchange between participants and the staff, who function not only as consultants but also as researchers.

Most major religious groups, of course, have developed their own approach to character education. Many national service organizations such as the Scouts, the 4-H Clubs, Boys' Clubs, Camp Fire Girls, and the like are greatly interested and concerned about such education. Their programs are in part designed to inculcate values of responsibility, concern, and respect for others as well as personal development. Thus, it would be inaccurate to say that values and character have been ignored or that materials and approaches are lacking. It is only that most of this work is divorced from the educational framework.

One notable exception is found in the schools run by the Ethical Culture Society. This group believes in ethical principles but does not believe in a personal god. As part of this belief, they provide courses in ethics for their students. What is taught depends largely on the teacher, but the focus is on the resolution of ethical dilemmas.

While these illustrations are interesting and perhaps encouraging, they do not represent a major entrance of ethical issues into the typical school curriculum or an attempt to cultivate ethical principles as a part of the general educational experience.

Applications

One of the basic principles developed and tested by the Character Research Project is "goal setting." Goal setting requires that the individual set for himself a practical goal that he can realize in the near future, preferably the same day. After the time period has elapsed, he records what has happened and briefly analyzes why it happened. His experience may then be discussed with a group of people who are also involved in goal setting.

This procedure lends itself to use in conjunction with homework assignments. For any given assignment, students can set goals about how they will study the material. These decisions must be individual, in keeping with the strengths, weaknesses, and schedules of the students involved.

One student might decide immediately to read through the material, then study it in detail on arriving home. Another might decide to do nothing. A third might decide to go over the material with a friend. Each would record in a notebook what he has done, how it worked, and any observations about what he learned in the process. The next day five minutes might be allowed for students to report on their experiences. The value of this process is that it turns homework into a learning experience on a different level. It encourages an orderly and responsible approach to the fulfillment of tasks, which is a prime prerequisite to any ethical development. It turns an imposed task into a source of helpful information.

A second area in which ethical considerations can be related to classroom activities is in the area of generating motivation to learn. A recent theme is "doing your own thing." One perversion of this theme is not doing anything unless you want to. Although students are not usually given much choice in the matter, there are moments in which a decision to give up or to make greater efforts toward an end is of great importance. At these times the definition of the relation between personal and social goals is of particular importance. For example:

We have just finished the first section of Introductory French. It is a good time to pause for a minute before we go on. Some of you have faithfully done everything that was asked of you. Some have done almost nothing. Most of you have done what you thought was necessary to get through. I suppose all this will be reflected in your marks, though this isn't always the case.

If you really want to do well, you have no problem. You will try hard. But most of you, I suspect, don't care that much. If you didn't have to learn French, you wouldn't bother. Obviously someone out there thinks it will do you good. Maybe that is important to you. Maybe it isn't. What I want you to think about is: "How can I get myself to do something I don't particularly want to do?" That is an important question. One of the differences between successful and unsuccessful people is that successful people know an answer to that question.

"What good does it do us to do what we don't want to do."

"I could give you an answer, but that wouldn't be *your* answer."

"What do you want us to do?"

"I want you to think. Do you agree with me that being successful involves doing unpleasant things?"

"I never thought about it."

"Think about it now. Where would you be if your parents did only what they wanted to do?"

"Don't they?"

"If parents really did just what they wanted to do, there probably wouldn't be many families around."

"My mother loves me."

"Love isn't enough. Sometimes when you are very annoying, she probably hates you. If she did what she felt like then, she might just send you away to live with some relatives."

"I thought there were laws about that."

"There are. Parents have no choice. They have to take care of their kids. But nothing can make them do a good job if they don't want to. Something else is necessary. They have to occasionally be able to go against themselves and do things they don't want to do.

A Class in Ethics

There are a variety of approaches that could be adopted in a class devoted to the cultivation of ethical values. One method is to study significant situations, each of which contains ethical conflicts—a student observing his friend cheating on an exam, a teacher favoring a student because she knows he has personal problems. Both students and teacher could supply these conflict situations. Group discussion would focus on behavior under the circumstance, seeking to deepen the individual's understanding of the situation and to develop greater tolerance and appreciation for alternate views. This approach would help the student to reconsider his own views and separate the automatic, unquestioned aspects of his beliefs from the more vital core that has been verified through experience.

Another method is through role playing standard conflict situations involving ethical considerations. This technique adds the behavioral dimension, so students can see how what people say and what they do may not be consistent. Ethics must be raised to the level of behavior if it is to have an important impact on the life of the individual.

A further approach could be to have the students write journals recounting some of the ethical conflicts and resolutions that occur in their daily lives. In addition the class might read and discuss ethical values of great men of the past.

A different approach would be systematically to relate ethical values to standard situations and conflicts. For example, students could determine under what conditions killing, stealing, lying, attacking, and the like would be acceptable and analyze the basic principles underlying such decisions.

Finally, they could study how to come to ethical decisions in situations in which they truly did not know what to do. For such situations exercises in creativity, visualization, empathy, and intellectual effort might be helpful in clarifying the problems involved and help to relate ethical values to other aspects of the curriculum.

CHAPTER ELEVEN

ATTENDING AND THE WILL

THE principal means of attaining control over one's organism is through selective attention and willing. There are certain conditions, such as being well-rested, that make the act of willing easier to perform. But the concept of willing is partially independent of the circumstances in which the act occurs.

Willing and attending are closely related to the act of choice. We cannot choose among alternatives if we do not realize they exist; we must attend in order to know. This understanding is a necessary but not sufficient condition for selection. The choice is an act of will, distinguished from other acts by the circumstances that have made it possible and by its strategic placement in a network of other actions that will follow from it after it has occurred. Just as a composer is constrained by his themes once he has selected them, so is the ordinary person limited when he has chosen among several alternatives that present themselves to him at a crossroads. But the ability to be at a crossroads in the first place and to make a productive choice when there, depend on attention and will. Attention helps us to realize when we are there and volition enables us to make the choice.

Our ability to pursue chosen goals irrespective of obstacles placed in our path is one measure of our freedom. Unless such motivated action is possible we are at the mercy of outer circumstances—our environment, other people, our society. On the other hand a person who ignores these influences is not necessarily free. He may simply be driven by a strong inner compulsion.

The less dependent we are upon immediate gratification, the more easily we can make the best choice. Fear of retribution is not enough. The person who is afraid may not perform overt evil acts but only because of the possible consequences to himself. If the fear is removed, he may be capable of anything. The only man who can be trusted is the one who can command himself. For this to be possible a man must know what he is facing and have the power to deal with it. These capabilities are evident in a successful ruler. They are less obvious and more necessary for the growing individual faced with balancing and utilizing the contradictory sides of his own nature.

Will training is generally associated with regimented situations such as military schools, political dictatorships, or survival training. The Spartans of ancient Greece specialized in such training to produce warriors who would be strong, merciless, and unafraid by rewarding them when they tolerated discomfort and pain. Certain American Indian tribes and Japanese Samurai warriors also underwent such training to give the individual mastery over bodily and emotional discomforts. The Indian system of Hatha Yoga performs a similar function. In modern life this theme has been pursued by the Outward Bound movement in England and the United States.[1] Teenage boys are taken into primitive and demanding environments where they must function at high levels of efficiency in order to survive. This experience produces an enhanced sense of competence and mastery over oneself and the environment.

In a different context a number of approaches to psychotherapy have placed heavy emphasis on the development of the will of the sick individual. Even Freud, who had little faith in the strength of the human ego, viewed one outcome of a successful psychoanalysis as the achievement of greater frustration tolerance. One reason that he abandoned hypnotism as a means of recovering early memories was his discovery that the slower psychotherapeutic process of recovering forgotten and repressed experiences was as important as the content of the experience. The process of overcoming resistance strengthened the individual, enabled him to handle the repressed material, and developed his will. When frustrating and difficult actions occurred in the future, the patient could use the courage and strength gained in psychoanalysis to meet the new threats and challenges.

Other therapists approach the matter more directly. For example, Dr. Abraham Low has utilized will training in a group context to help mental patients adjust to community responsibilities.[2] In Low's approach elaborate theoretical statements are ignored. Depth interpretations are avoided. He focuses on symptoms and the maneuvers in which patients engage in order to avoid improvement. His efforts are directed toward two kinds of actions—showing the patients how they are sabotaging the therapeutic process, and helping them to learn to spot the emergence of symptoms as quickly as possible so that they can take immediate corrective action against them.

This approach underplays the patient's sense of helplessness before his difficulties and emphasizes what he can do, both by himself and in relation with others who either have experienced or are experiencing his kinds of difficulties. Responsibility is shifted onto the individual, as it must be for any kind of will training. The group provides support, but it cannot make him act any more than a mother can force a child to eat.

A more elaborate process of training the will is contained in the psychosynthesis approach to personal development.[3] Psychosynthesis was created by an Italian psychiatrist, Dr. Robert Assagioli, in an effort to integrate physical, mental, emotional, and spiritual approaches to personal growth. The application of will power has a prominent place. According to Assagioli, there are five stages involved in the training of the will. In the first the individual starts with a purpose or aim. Having formulated the aim, he experiences intent within himself to achieve it. This intent must be related to his motivations, conscious or unconscious. These motivations must be evaluated by whatever ethical principles the individual employs. Finally, he must deliberate about the relation between his principles, intent, motivation, and original purpose. In the second stage the individual makes a choice among alternatives. He decides what he will do. In the third stage, closely following the second, he affirms his decision. He tells himself that "it will be." This affirmation may have to be repeated from time to time as the need arises. In the fourth stage he must outline a practical plan of activities designed to achieve his goal. If necessary, he will outline a set of interrelated stages each of which is necessary to enable him to reach his ultimate intent. The fifth stage involves execution of the plan and requires two different qualities—first, concentrated attention to the given task, and second, ability to persist.

A number of practical approaches to training the will are utilized in psychosynthesis. In one exercise the individual is asked to relax and then recall unfortunate consequences of lack of will power in the past. Then he pictures the various benefits to himself and others of having will power. Finally, he visualizes himself as possessing will power and attaining desired ends.

Another approach is to perform useless exercises for no other purpose than the strengthening of will. This might consist of exercising a group of muscles, walking the long way around to arrive at a given location, denying oneself something that one would like, or enduring a slight physical discomfort. Alternative approaches are controlling one's temper, moving slowly even when in a hurry, or going to bed at a precise time. Gymnastics are useful if they are faithfully practiced. Cultivation of constructive personal habit can be a testing ground for the development of the will, independent of the benefits that the habit itself may bring to the possessor.

Applications

When students become convinced of the importance of will power in attaining their own ends, they can adopt many educational tasks to cultivate their will. This orientation might be introduced as follows:

If you are lucky, some of the things you want simply come to you without any effort on your part, such as a present that you had hoped to get for Christmas. But most of the time you have to work for what you get.

There are three stages to getting what you want. The first is to be able to visualize it. You must be able to imagine yourself as already having it. The second step is to make a plan for obtaining what you have imagined. The third and crucial step is acting on your plan. This requires will power. You must focus your attention on what you have to do to the exclusion of everything else. And you must stick to it even if you forget why you started or begin to doubt that you really want whatever it is that waits at the end. The power to concentrate and the power to endure are the keys to success. No inventor, no statesman, no religious leader ever succeeded without these qualities.

The reason I mention this is that as you do your work in school and at home you can develop your concentration and your persistence. You are going to have to do the work in any case. But if you do it right, you can learn these valuable qualities at the same time.

But how can this happen? There are some simple things you can do. First, you can establish a schedule and stick to it as if your life depended on it. At a certain hour every day you can sit down and do homework, whether you feel like it or not. This takes discipline and will power. After you have done it for a while it will become a habit and you will want to do it. Then you will have to find something else on which to practice. You can decide never to eat supper unless you have done a certain subject that you don't like. You can go over your math once more than you usually do looking for mistakes. You can go to bed at a definite time.

Pick things that are useful in themselves and that you

don't want to do. Then do them! It sounds simple, but it certainly isn't easy. However, there is no other way to learn how to control yourself except to do it a little bit at a time. Each success gives you more strength. Each failure makes it more difficult the next time. Think about it and then tomorrow we can take the next step—selecting something definite to work on.

One of the most important aspects of learning anything is placing one's attention on it. If one is daydreaming, distracted, or dazed, one cannot perceive, much less think about any material that is being presented. One must be alert, and one must concentrate on the matter at hand. If one does not start a task in a concentrating state, it is hard to attain it as one goes along unless the subject matter is inherently interesting. An exercise in concentration can be helpful. Specifically, an individual can focus on the teacher's voice, the objects in the room, or his own heartbeat to eliminate distracting thoughts.

A different approach is to have the individual frequently shift the focus of his attention so that it becomes more flexible. This might occur as follows:

> Before we continue our work I want to go through a brief exercise with you. Imagine your arms stretched above your head. See them as vividly as you can. Now slowly allow your arms actually to raise themselves up. Keep the image clear. Let your arms be drawn up by the image. When they are all the way up, imagine them sideways, but keep them up. Imagine them sideways more vividly and then allow them to move in that position if they want to. Now relax. . . . Next, imagine yourself making a funny face. See the face as if you were standing in front of yourself looking at it. See it vividly. Then let your face take on the expression that you imagine, if it wants to. . . . Now let it all go. Now imagine yourself sitting quietly without a thought in your head. Without losing the picture, allow yourself actually to be that way. Now let that go and we will get to work.

A final means of introducing will training exercises into the learning situation involves the use of calculated distractions. In the usual study period, for example, some effort is made to create a quiet atmosphere. This makes concentration easier by eliminating competing sources of interest. Suppose a study hall or a library were turned into bedlam, all in an effort to distract the student from the work on which he was concentrating. To endure such a situation the student would have to utilize the full force of his power of concentration, which he might do if he looked on the situation around him as a challenge he was seeking to overcome.

For practical purposes five minutes out of an hour might be turned over to such a process, some of the students studying while the others seek to disturb or distract them. Instructions might be as follows:

> When I give the signal, I want all the students in the center row to keep on studying regardless of what happens. Do it as if your life depended on it. The rest of you can do anything you want to distract them except touch them physically or take their books away. Anything else is permissible. Say anything you want. Make any gestures. Your objective is to prevent them from studying. Is everyone ready? I will signal when five minutes are up. BEGIN!
>
> Five minutes are up. Could you concentrate at all? If you could, then you know that you are capable of getting work done under the worst conditions if you really are willing to make the effort. It is just a matter of training and motivation. Tomorrow the row on the right can be the focus of attention.

A Class in Willing

How can the will be cultivated? One approach is through learning to tolerate pain. Various exercises in Hatha Yoga would be useful in this regard. They put the body in unusual and uncomfortable positions. Learning to stay in these positions can be done only through strong effort of will. A quite different approach has been developed by the Outward Bound Program of Survival Training, mentioned earlier. Although this program, which takes youth of varied backgrounds into the wilderness, is intended to help them develop their potential for survival and growth, its primary ingredient is will training. The participant forces himself to do things he did not believe possible—rock climbing, living off the forest, diving into icy waters. The spirit of the group and the organization of the experience heighten his motivation to do difficult and unpleasant things, but these would be insufficient without great individual efforts. This experience by definition cannot be conducted in the classroom but there is no reason that it has to be. Prescott College, for example, devotes part of its Freshman Orientation to survival training in mountain wilderness.

On the other hand there are ways of teaching tolerance of pain that can be used in the classroom. For example, students can practice tolerating very mild and then slightly stronger electric shocks. The equipment for generating electricity can sometimes be found in the science department where an experiment sometimes used is to have students form a circle with hands touching as a mild electric current is passed around the circle to illustrate conduction. Or they can stand with the arms extended for ten minutes or more. Any simple standard experience involving the overcoming of pain and discomfort is suitable for the training of will on the physical level.

With the great emphasis upon intellectual achievement that exists it is surprising that more attention has not been given to the relation of will to thought. Perhaps this is owing to the primary emphasis being placed on the external product rather than the individual's intellectual processes. Most people do not realize that they cannot completely control their own thoughts. The process of focusing thoughts on a given object and keeping them there is a very rare occurrence. Most of our waking experience is a series of impressions that flash through our awareness in a semi-twilight state. Often we do not even know what we are thinking. It goes on all by itself.

The ability to focus the mind on a given object or to eliminate thoughts altogether requires special approaches. The methods for producing such an extension of will are most clearly found in Raja Yoga and other systems of con-centration. The work of Sadhu mentioned in connection with perception is also useful.

In the emotional domain a well proven approach to de-veloping the will is through undertaking tasks of increasing difficulty. This method has been used in psychotherapy and lends itself well to classroom activity. The student is given a set of graded tasks of increasing difficulty. For example, if he finds it hard to relate to others, he might begin by talking to one stranger in the hall; go on to talking with several; later be given a week to develop a new friend; a little later be re-quired to give a party, etc.

This approach in conjunction with the others that have been mentioned should provide a powerful collection of methods for the training of the will on the physical, emo-tional and intellectual levels.

CHAPTER TWELVE

MEDITATION

A bewildering array of methods for meditating use contrasting or even opposing approaches for achieving similar ends. Some methods require that thoughts be eliminated, others that they be fixed on a single object, and still others that they be formed into a daydream. Nevertheless, all approaches share certain common assumptions that help distinguish meditation from other human activities.

Meditation is typically quiet. If actions are involved, they are usually gentle in nature. The most observable characteristic of a meditating person is that he adopts a given pose and keeps it as long as the meditation continues. The pose may be the traditional lotus position of the Buddha or may involve nothing more than sitting comfortably on a straight-back chair. Meditation requires the conscious control of attention. The object of attention may vary, but all methods demand that the person must be on guard to avoid losing the particular focus he has undertaken to hold. Any method of meditation requires patient and regular practice if its intended effects are to be experienced. It cannot be performed in a haphazard manner.

The study of meditation in Western society is generally limited to members of certain religious orders who combine

it with intensive visualization experiences. In the East meditation is more accessible to interested laymen in a variety of
forms. One can find it integrated with painting, flower arranging, sports, systems of self-defense, sexual intercourse,
and music.

It is rare for most people to experience the spontaneous
single-pointed focus on an activity to the exclusion of all others that characterizes successful meditative practice. Yet, just
such clarity is extremely useful in learning and performing a
variety of tasks. Thus, the practice of meditation might be extremely useful in preparing the individual for the learning
process and aiding him in making it more efficient.

Westerners tend to feel that meditation is somehow foreign or unreal. They picture it as an activity that removes one
from life. This stereotype is understandable, but it is quite incorrect. The principle tool possessed by any individual is his
own attention. Unless he can gain some mastery over its
function he is at the mercy of whatever stimuli impinge upon
him. By learning consciously to direct his awareness he can
learn to balance and control the impact of the forces of his
inner or outer environment. He can create within himself a
quiet place from which he can view with sympathetic dispas-
sion the reality that surrounds him. However, the emphasis
on control should not be taken to imply that attention is to
be forced. Awareness is a subtle quality. It must be approached like a bird ready to take flight at the first alarm.

One of the simplest approaches to meditation, developed in Zen Buddhism, involves counting one's breaths. The
individual simply notes each complete breathing cycle,
counts up to ten such cycles and then begins over again. Attention is placed in the lower abdomen during this practice.
The exercise may continue anywhere from ten minutes to a
half an hour, depending on the experience of the practitioner.
As a variant the individual may stand and slowly walk
around the room, still counting his breaths and keeping his
center of attention in his lower abdomen.

The very simplicity of this approach is one of its chief
advantages. Its general effect is to quiet the individual. It

gives him the opportunity to sink more deeply into his own experience of himself and to store up energy that might otherwise be expended in tension and unproductive thought.

A sharply contrasting method involves "doing nothing." In this approach the individual views himself from the vantage point of an observer. All the usual activities with which he identifies himself are looked at with objectivity. He notes his actions, thoughts, feelings, and sensations with an air of equanimity and detachment. He observes and experiences them for what they are and recognizes that they are not himself but simply what he experiences.

No attempt is made to influence or control what is happening. The effort is solely on experiencing without identifying with the content of the experience. This orientation cannot be adopted all at once, though abruptly adopting the attitude that "everything that I experience is not me" may have a certain effect. Fundamentally, it must be approached by a continuing awareness of every aspect of experience . . . a thought . . . a feeling . . . a sensation . . . each following the other in a continuous panorama of events each of which is recognized and each of which is identified as "not I."

This method is essentially a process of introspection, the purpose of which is not so much self-knowledge and self-understanding, but penetration that finally centers in an area of consciousness where the "I" exists. But this "I" is not the same as the individual personality. It is the ground within which conscious events are placed and the necessary condition of their actualization. This form of awareness meditation is most clearly developed in Hinayana Buddhism, but elements of the practice are found in most major religions.

A third type of meditation involves the shifting of identity through concentration. It is closely related to willing in that it emphasizes an unbroken focus upon a particular object. Without control over thoughts, feelings, and sensations the individual cannot succeed in this approach. The major difference between such meditation and simple willing is in the object toward which the concentration is directed. The

ordinary person usually selects a personal goal such as success, love, or power as the focus of his attention. In meditation the focus is typically on a holy object, image, or person.
By placing his attention on the level of existence to which he
aspires, the person in meditation approaches this level, at
least temporarily. As the focus becomes more intense and the
practice more complete, the influence of the higher level becomes more pervasive.

A fourth approach to meditation involves the use of
visualization. In many ways this approach is similar to shifting the identity through concentration. It differs mainly in
that no real object exists as the focus of attention. The individual concentrates on an image or a sensation. The image
may be static or in motion. The effort is to perceive it vividly
and continuously. Again, a holy symbol is usually selected,
though the basic process is not fundamentally different from
that of creative artists or inventors who become obsessed
with a product they are creating. They can't put it down.
They are drawn to it, as a lover is drawn to the image of his
beloved. When this stage is reached, it does not require any
particular effort to maintain the focus of attention. It takes
more effort to let go of the image than to hold it, but before
this degree of interest and involvement is generated a long
preliminary period of effort is necessary.

The visualization may exist in empty space or it may be
related to a part of the physical organism. The individual
may be asked to see a color or a shape in a particular part in
his body. The purpose of such an exercise is to awaken latent
functions in the body that are presumed to reside in specific
locations. But whether the image shifts or is held constant,
whether it is in empty space or within the individual, the
power of concentration on a selected objective is always required.

A fifth form of meditation utilizes a combination of
guided daydream and sensory awareness. In its spontaneous
form this approach constitutes mystical experience. The individual sees visions that are the equivalent of waking dreams.
They differ principally in their content and quality, i.e., they

have a celestial or demonic content and may produce ecstatic emotional states.

In its more systematic aspect the individual may be encouraged consciously to initiate a visionary experience which, if he is fortunate, may lead into a spontaneous occurrence. Guided daydreams may be encouraged by providing an initial stimulus such as a door that is to be opened or a mountain that is to be climbed. From this beginning the individual allows an inner fantasy to occur which he experiences as he would a dream.

Other approaches emphasize an awareness of a great force, such as the air, sunlight, or the darkness of space that spreads into vast distances. As the person experiences this vastness, he may be led into an experience that goes beyond the immediate medium with which he is identifying.

In other cases he may experience some physiological process that has religious significance, such as his own death and dissolution. A fine line exists between an inner psychological experience of personal significance to the individual, such as an insight into unconscious material, and a religious experience in which the person's relation to some cosmic power is redefined. From a practical point of view, the distinction is not important. If the individual has a strong visionary experience in relation to that which is "not I," it is likely to have a strong impact on his own goals and his experience of himself. Regardless of its point of origin, it can provide important motivation for the pursuit of growth, which is the pragmatic test of the value of any such event.

Applications

As previously indicated, motivation for learning can be enhanced if the student identifies with the subject matter. Meditation provides a direct and effective method for heightening such identification. For example:

> In a few minutes I am going to discuss this book which you have all been assigned. Before I begin I am going to put it

here on my desk. I want you to look at it. For the next few minutes all you have to do is concentrate on the book. Don't think about it. Just be aware of it. Put all your attention on it. In the whole world, the only real thing for you will be this book. Begin now. I will tell you when to stop.

My own experience has been that when students concentrate in this manner on any object it may come alive for many of them and take on a perceptual vividness and emotional concern that lasts for many minutes after the experience is concluded.

A related approach is to have students focus on the portrait of someone whom they admire and who stands for the kinds of educational objectives the teacher wishes to develop. Focusing attention on such a picture helps the students to experience some of the qualities that the living person embodied, just as meditating on the figure of Christ helps the religious Christian to rediscover his own sense of dedication to the ideals proclaimed and illustrated by Christ in his own lifetime.

A related use of meditation involves reenergizing the student or teacher after a concentrated period of attention. In this instance one might focus on a beautiful relaxing situation.

Meditation may be of use in the mastery of material viewed as particularly difficult by students. In such circumstances students tend to become defensive and their performance suffers. In such a situation a "not I" form of meditation may help to restore their sense of proportion as follows:

> If you are getting discouraged or frightened by this new subject matter, I want to suggest an exercise that may help. Stop what you are doing for a moment and just observe what is going on inside you. Experience each thing that occurs, whether it is a thought, a feeling, a sensation, or a perception. Realize what it is and realize also that it is not you but only something you experience. If you start to daydream, bring yourself back to an awareness of your inner experience. Try it for a minute or two on your own. Afterward you may feel bet-

ter able to understand the new material with which we are dealing.

A simple application of meditation to the enhancement of the learning process is to have the student focus for a few minutes on the teacher, seeking to experience him as fully as possible. After such an experience the teacher will probably be sensed in a more vivid manner. Anything he says or does will be more directly perceived and will have a greater effect. The principle is the same as focusing on a glass of water. However, when one concentrates on another human being, a persistent feeling of connectedness is created between the viewer and the person being perceived. Listening to the other becomes like listening to oneself. Instructions for such an exercise are simple.

> For the next few minutes I want you to do something you do most of the time anyway. I want you to look at me. Only this time I want you to focus all your energy on experiencing me. Put every bit of attention you can muster on that. Nothing else exists in the world. Only me! Try to absorb me so fully that you forget about yourself. I am going to sit here quietly. Start when you are ready. I'll tell you when the time is up.

A Class in Meditation

There are well developed Western and Eastern systems for the practice of meditation. Perhaps the most carefully developed Western system is that of St. Ignatius Loyola in which the aspirant relives the life of Christ through a series of guided visualizations. The content would not be appropriate for a classroom, but the basic pattern could be followed utilizing subject matter such as the life of a famous person or a historical event.

There are many eastern systems of meditation: Jnana Yoga, Raja Yoga, Tantric Yoga, Taoism, and various Buddhist approaches. Each of these is the basis of a way of life. The problem is one of selection rather than availability.

An interesting series of exercises that might be used in a meditation class is given by Paul Brunton in his book *The Wisdom of the Overself*.[1] He describes seven forms of meditation that he learned during his extensive travels throughout the Orient. The first is performed either at sunrise or twilight. The student sits in an open position and allows the rays of the rising or setting sun to penetrate into his organism through his eyes. He allows the cosmic change that is happening in front of him to become part of his own experience. Slowly, as he identifies with the light, he becomes the light spreading throughout the universe.

A second exercise involves reliving the past. In the evening before sleep the student relives the day, working backward until he reaches the same point in the day of the previous evening. He sees every scene as vividly and impersonally as possible. A third exercise is to anticipate the future. In the evening before sleep the student anticipates the precise form of an event that he expects to occur on the following day. He tries to visualize it as clearly as if it had already happened and to have it take a form which is beneficial both for himself and those around him.

A fourth exercise in this series differs from the others in that it does not require special conditions for undertaking it. The student simply and abruptly takes the attitude of one who suddenly wakes from a dream. He holds to his attitude as strongly as possible for several minutes allowing all surrounding events to continue without him. He becomes a detached observer.

A fifth meditation involves gaining control over one's night time dreams. In the beginning this takes the form of the student strongly suggesting to himself, while still awake, that as he falls asleep he will be aware that he is dreaming. This may not meet with any immediate success, but slowly he may come into a more direct relation to his dream life. If he persists he may slowly have the experience of extending his conscious awareness of himself into the dreaming state. The dream will occur, and the person will know that it is happening. He will observe it but not be in it. If and when this occurs, the activities of the night will turn into something like an extended guided daydream and in this way open up an area of human experience that is usually lost for direct productive work of any kind. There is a striking similarity between this approach and the "dream" method of astral projection described by Ophiel.

A sixth meditation concerns sleep itself. It focuses on capturing the instant when wakefulness shifts into sleep. This transition may be heralded by a changing physical awareness. The student may lose consciousness of his legs, his body, and finally his head. At a certain neutral point the crucial change of consciousness occurs. If the student can seize that flash according to Brunton he can experience consciousness in its purest form.

A final meditation utilizes the same principle but in the waking state. The student attempts to experience the interval between thoughts, just as one might observe the paper between written words. This requires him to concentrate completely on his mental experience, not for purposes of analyzing its content but to uncover its discontinuities.

Each of the foregoing methods provides different kinds of experiences and benefits. All require extended practice to be effective, and ordinarily a student works on only one of them at a time. Collectively they represent only a small sampling of the varied approaches that are available in this area of experience.

CHAPTER THIRTEEN

ROLE BEHAVIOR

THE process of socializing the young to play appropriate roles is conducted through selective reward and punishment of behaviors with which the child experiments, largely in play. He must have the freedom to experiment, but he must also have parental and peer group reaction to his performance. This experience tends to produce persons who are able to perform those actions required by society. Such training is necessary for the survival of institutions within which these roles are enacted. It also produces some measure of predictability in social behavior without which we would live in uncertainty and anxiety. The individual pays a price for these useful social attributes. He limits what he does and alienates himself from the full range of his possible actions by artificially compartmentalizing his experience and hiding unsocialized aspects of himself from others. This strategy is usually only partially successful. Periodically, the individual may break out in behavior destructive to himself and others as a partial relief from his burden of unexpressed tendencies. He may resort to drink, drugs, orgies, or he may perform direct antisocial acts. Through these activities he finds temporary relief from his chronic state of role starvation but no permanent solution.

The development of human potentiality involves the expansion of the range and quality of human experience, i.e., extending the kinds of role performances available to the individual. Life is not long enough nor society strong enough to allow even the adventurous individual to experience all or even most of the roles he is capable of performing. Those who try are penalized by others whom they threaten and sources of institutional support are revoked. This may be an understandable reaction from society, but it is not good from the viewpoint of the individual interested in his own growth and development.

Whether we are concerned with the child and young adolescent learning to become adults or the individual at any stage who wishes to grow beyond himself, the cultivation of role performance must occupy a central position. It involves the self but is objective. It involves the group but is situational. It constitutes a meeting ground for social scientists, artists, and those interested in personal and social change.

In view of the importance of role behavior, it is remarkable how little direct effort is made in the educational curriculum to train persons in even socially approved roles. The student learns to play the role of the student and a few other roles, such as peer group member and dating partner, but these roles are not consciously taught. The student picks them up in the course of daily activity. He does not participate in any experience that teaches him fundamental social roles in the way the actor is taught to enact complex stage roles, through rehearsal, analysis, and the relation of his own experience and personality to the character being studied. This is a remarkable loss since, at minimum, education is supposed to prepare the individual to take a place in society.

If education completely loses sight of its role cultivation function, it becomes trivial or meaningless. If it looks on students simply as material to be molded into a set of preassigned patterns, it becomes mechanical. Only when education offers the student the opportunity to experiment with alternate possibilities, to test through experience their own potential, can it serve not only a social function but the personal one of aiding the individual to cultivate his capacities.

There are numerous approaches to the training of role performances. Perhaps the simplest and most widely utilized is "role playing," a procedure originated by Dr. J. L. Moreno in the course of his work on the development of psychodrama.[1] Role playing involves the performance of a social role in a specified situation without a script. The participants are typically non-actors seeking to increase their understanding of and competence in performing the roles. This approach is based on the principle that the best way to learn is to become that which one wishes to understand. Role playing has been used in varied sets of circumstances, often by people who do not know its origins or precisely what it is intended to achieve. It has been applied in industry, government, the armed forces, psychotherapy, and of course, education.

Other approaches to the teaching of roles are available, most of them developed in the context of actor training. One set of such exercises is called theater games, developed by Viola Spolin.[2] Although these games were developed to train actors, they have been applied to other situations and are suitable for students of all ages interested in extending the range of their behavior.

In the strictest sense theater games do not teach role performance. Rather, they develop the separate capacities that are needed to perform complex stage roles, either one at a time or in various combinations. For example, the game of moving in slow motion is primarily related to physical action. Having an imaginary tug of war involves sensory, physical, and social components. Theater games always require that the individual do at least two things at once. Thus, he may be instructed to touch another person every time he talks to him, or to change the nature of his reaction every time a certain word is spoken. In this manner he learns to divide his attention, to be in the game and somewhere else at the same time. These games teach the skills underlying flexible and successful social behavior while not directly trying to train the behavior itself, as in role playing.

Applications

The major contributions that role training methods have made to education is through the technique of role playing. All educational material is meant to be used in at least one situation other than the class itself in which it is presented; otherwise, there can be little justification for teaching it. This other situation can be brought to life through role playing, thus increasing the usefulness of the material and aiding in the transfer of learning that must be the ultimate objective of any educational experience. This projection of future application can be either realistic or fanciful, depending on the needs of the situation. A realistic projection might involve a time when the student of French is visiting France or the student of Spanish is working with slum children from Puerto Rico. A fanciful projection might place a student of physics on the moon in order to enhance his need to understand the operation of physical laws in such a situation. Applications of this sort are both important and endless.

A second form of utilizing role playing in presenting educational material involves role reversal. The student becomes the teacher and the teacher the student. Beneficial aspects of this technique include that it helps each appreciate the role of the other and it heightens the student's involvement in the educational process. In fact, the teacher usually learns more than anyone else in the class. Why should the student be barred from the benfits of such an experience? This approach is to be distinguished from the more nondirective and progressive orientation in which the teacher steps down and the class as a social unit decides on what it will do and how it will do it. Role playing simply involves an alternation of who is playing which role.

A third aspect of this form of application is in relation to the materials to be studied. This is probably the most central concern of the traditional educator. He wants students to increase their knowledge and understanding of facts and ideas. Role playing can aid by involving the students' behavior, emotions, thoughts, and creativity in the learning process, a process which is usually only verbal and intellectual.

As previously suggested in the discussion of empathy, role playing need not be limited to human situations. It can involve animals and plants, organic and inorganic compounds. A student who has portrayed the growth process of a plant or a tree will be more interested in the study of botany than ever before, if his portrayal is done with sufficient detail and intensity. In addition to making the material more alive, taking the part of the other helps the student to realize the areas of his ignorance and at the same time motivates him to do something about it. If he starts to grow as a seed in a role playing situation and then realizes he does not know how far his root grows before his head appears above the ground, he will have a motivation to find out. The biological issue has been brought into his own life.

We can conceive of a curriculum of situations in which every subject matter is defined in terms of key situations involving the materials of the content area that could be explored through role playing. Such a curriculum does not exist, but its possibilities are intriguing. Although role playing has been applied as a teaching device to a wide variety of subject matter, its inherent potency has not yet been appreciated or fully utilized.

A second major use of role playing in the educational process is for role training. Whenever the curriculum is intended to prepare the individual to take a particular social role, giving him the opportunity to play the role under controlled conditions is obviously the most direct approach.

Role training and simulation have much in common. The military and NASA employ extensive simulation techniques, having realized that the best way to train men for emergency situations for which they are unprepared is to create a realistic counterpart in which these contingencies can be rehearsed. In role training less attention is given to the physical authenticity of outer detail than in simulation, but the basic principle is identical. Whether the educational program is devoted to training for technical, professional, family roles, a powerful way to approach the task is to put people in situations in which they will be called on to perform the given roles under conditions in which practice is possible.

A third major application of role playing to the educational process is in studying and solving problem situations that occur in the educational setting. There is a vast number of such situations surrounding the educational enterprise. To list only a few:

1. Taking a test.
2. Going against the group norm when it conflicts with one's personal beliefs.
3. Maintaining order in the classroom.
4. Lack of communication between administrators, teachers, students, and parents.
5. Conflicts between ethical principles and actual practices.
6. Lack of student motivation to study important but uninteresting material.
7. Controversy surrounding the introduction of programs such as sex education.

Any such problem can be examined through the vehicle of role playing to increase the level of understanding of the issues involved and to explore alternative solutions in a realistic but creative manner.

A Class in Role Behavior

A good case could be made for training in role playing as the most vital aspect of the educational experience. If a person can perform effectively in a variety of key life situations, his personal success is largely assured. The technical aspects of many jobs can be quickly learned, but the ability to move smoothly from one style of action to another, and the ability to act appropriately in a given situation are crucial elements in successful attainment.

Performing a role is a complex integrated action involving most or all of the other human capacities. In a different sense it constitutes an opportunity to translate into meaningful social action the heightened awareness and technical competence attained in the other classes. Further, the opportunity to play roles that are not ordinarily performed or to rehearse new ones before they need to be performed is an immensely important aspect of the development of latent capacities.

It is a reasonable working hypothesis that very few people are given the opportunity to fulfill their potential role repertoire. Social institutions simply do not offer sufficient opportunity for role flexibility and fix great penalties on any significant deviation from role prescriptions. The young child is more fortunate. He is able in play to perform all kinds of actions that for the adult would lead to disapproval and criminal prosecution. He learns about society by playing at the various roles that he conceives to lie within it. Only actors and other creative types are allowed such leeway as adults, and then only when it is clearly understood that their actions are limited to certain areas such as a stage or a canvas.

Whether we adopt the view of society that persons need to perform assigned roles effectively and shift efficiently from role to role as the situational context alters, or the view of the individual seeking self-understanding and personal growth, the need to develop an expanded role repertoire is clear. The most systematic manner in which to approach this task is to develop a system for analyzing the basic aspects of any role performance. Several important variables in such an analytic system would be status, sex, age, and feeling tone. Working with only these four variables a variety of different role performances can be developed. For example, consider a relation involving equal status, different sexes, similar ages, and varied feeling tones. This would consist of a couple whose feelings for each other could be any on the following chart.

Each of these possibilities represents real, important human situations. For example, situation one involves a mutual romantic attraction; situation six concerns an indifferent man relating to a woman who dislikes him (e.g., the woman might be the best friend of his girl friend, jealous of his relationship with her.) A well developed individual needs to be

		Male	Female
Possibility	1.	+	+
"	2.	+	0
"	3.	+	−
"	4.	0	+
"	5.	0	0
"	6.	0	−
"	7.	−	+
"	8.	−	0
"	9.	−	−

KEY

+ = love
0 = indifference
− = hate

able to handle all these situations, whether they characterize different aspects of a single ongoing relationship or several different ones. They cover in abstract form the major aspects of relationships between men and women of the same age and status. It seems clear that the four basic dimensions of age, sex, status, and feeling tones are sufficient to generate enough roles to occupy much class time and involve many essential aspects of human interaction. A student who was able to successfully perform in situations that describe all the various combinations and permutations of these fundamental variables of human interaction could be viewed as having achieved an important aspect of successful role functioning.

There are yet other approaches to the training of role performance. The works of Spolin, Stanislavski, and Strasberg provide a number of methods both for the development of character and the freeing of the expressive function in the actor. Many techniques taught in most drama schools could be directly applied to this task. Particularly relevant is the work of Moreno who in 1924 in his Theater of Spontaneity carefully examined the challenges and opportunities of training individuals spontaneously to take any role required in an improvised play.

Moreno made an important distinction between psychological, social, and axiological roles. Psychological roles are the roles played by significant others who influence or have influenced the given individual. Social roles are positions in the institutional fabric—policemen, student, wife. Axiological roles exist in the cosmic sphere—angels, devils, spirits, nature, God. Whether one views such creations as figments of the creator's imagination or real beings, they exist as myths and exert influence both on the individual and the society of which he is a part. The fulfilled individual must be able to perform all roles; psychological, social, and axiological.

For this purpose the stage is a marvelous social invention. It is not practical for individuals to quickly extend their role repertoire within their normal life. Any such expansion must be worked through carefully in advance or it may create more difficulties than it resolves. The stage, however, is socially defined as a magical arena in which anything can occur but nothing is quite real, hence it is the ideal vehicle for social experimentation. For any class in role performance a stage is the ideal laboratory for focusing on the fundamental human situations and then extending the focus in the intrapersonal and cosmic realm as opportunity, motivation, and time permit.

CHAPTER FOURTEEN

CONDITIONING

M ANY theories of personality are based on the notion that an organism acts in such a way as to maximize pleasure and avoid pain. This premise is held by such diverse groups as objective behaviorists and depth psychotherapists. It also forms the core of many socialization practices. Few would quarrel that, other things being equal, people would rather feel good than bad, happy than sad, but there are many exceptions. People will kill themselves in the service of their country or starve themselves for a political cause or a personal belief. They will give up sexual contact for the sake of religious convictions. It is usually assumed that they do these things because of some greater good that the sacrifice may bring, but what is most striking is not that this may be the case, but rather that human behavior is capable of such modification for the attainment of goals that may be distant and whose realization cannot be assured.

One discovery that helps to explain the willingness to pursue courses of action that do not provide immediate gratification is the power of intermittent reinforcement. Studies of animals and humans have demonstrated that if an individual is inconsistently rewarded for a particular behavior, he will continue to perform it. Even if the reward ceases altogether he will persist in it for a long time. The reason for this tendency has not been explained, but its existence has been demonstrated repeatedly. Given this mechanism, much of the behavior in which we engage becomes explicable. At one time we are rewarded for some performance and on subsequent occasions the reward again follows. So we continue because the pattern has been established. It is fortunate that it is so, otherwise no one would ever learn to act in an expected or civilized manner. On the other hand, we can be victims of conditioning patterns that have ceased either to be functional or rewarding. Thus, a person who is in love with someone who has ceased to return the affection continues as a result of past rewards and may in the future attempt to duplicate the relation with someone similar to the person who has departed. Childlike habits that may have been appropriate at one age persist into another age even though they are inappropriate. Much pathological behavior can be interpreted in such a light. For example, neurotic defense mechanisms represent behaviors that occasionally worked in the past as means of handling anxiety-provoking behavior. What starts as a self-regulating mechanism preserving the integrity of the personality turns into a Frankenstein monster through intermittent reinforcement.

There are two major approaches to neutralizing this effect. The first is extinction. Failure to reward over a sufficiently long period results in the given behavior becoming less frequent and perhaps ceasing altogether. It is unlikely that extinction will occur by chance. The more probable situation is that intermittent reward will occasionally occur so that a special effort must be undertaken to avoid it.

The second approach is punishment. If a person is hurt physically, emotionally, or intellectually when he performs a certain act, the likelihood that he will persist is not great. Punishment tends to repress a behavior rather than extinguish it, so if the punishment ceases, the behavior reappears. Punishment is a better instrument of control than of change.

When an individual is punished for a given behavior, he tends to become anxious when a situation arises in which the same behavior might manifest itself. This effect is heightened if the same behavior is occasionally rewarded so that the individual does not know what to expect. This can occur quite frequently under normal circumstances because of the inconsistency of our standards and expectations. A person can anticipate that a given kind of behavior, such as cheating on an examination, may be punished by some individuals, such as the teacher, but tolerated by his peers. The prospect of both reward and punishment is anxiety-provoking. The individual tends to persist through reward but grows more frightened in the prospect of punishment. Such conditions have been used to create neurotic behavior in animals and probably have the same effect on human beings.

All of the preceding suggests that the use of reward and punishment needs to be administered on a more rational basis than is usually the case. Otherwise the right hand and the left hand work in opposition.

The systematic application of rewards and punishments for purposes of behavioral modification, although techniques may vary, is collectively described as "behavior therapy." This field of work is very active at the present, appealing principally to those who seek quick relief of symptoms and utilizing an approach that is based, at least indirectly, on scientific findings. Behavior therapy has been tried with virtually every kind of psychologically disturbed individual as well as those suffering from neurological deficiencies, such as brain damaged children, with generally encouraging results.

Although the variations in technique are almost endless, three principal methods are employed. The first is experimental extinction. If a particular response has been previously associated with a reward or a punishment, the effect of this conditioning will gradually be reduced if neither occurs after the given action has been taken. This principle underlies the use of "negative practice." Presuming that stuttering occurred originally because of some anxiety-arousing situation, a therapist will force a stutterer to stutter worse in a situation that is not anxiety arousing. In time the stuttering disappears. Similarly, if a person imagines often enough a situation of which he is afraid, the power of the situation to influence him is often diminished. He wears it out.

A second approach is counter-conditioning or reciprocal inhibition. If someone has formed a negative response to a given situation, this bond can be directly attacked by seeking to put a positive bond in its place. Pleasure is substituted for pain. This may take several forms. If a person is afraid of expressing certain emotions, he is encouraged to do so. If he represses his anger, he is encouraged to experience and express it within limits. This action helps to eliminate the accumulation of anxiety, which in itself constitutes a reward that reinforces such assertive actions once they have been undertaken.

Relaxation may also be used as a counter-conditioning agent. If a person can be trained to relax and then consciously relaxes in the presence of a fear-inducing situation, over a period of time he can change the situation from a fearful one to a pleasant one by controlling the emotion associated with it.

The reinforcing stimulus need not be positive. One can use an electric shock in order to create reciprocal inhibition. Thus, the treatment of compulsive habits by administering a punishment that makes the expression of the pathological behavior even more painful may lead the patient into giving up the symptom in order to avoid the shock. The cessation of shock constitutes the reward.

A third general principle is positive reconditioning. One seeks to develop desirable patterns of behavior by rewarding them when they occur while seeking to eliminate competing or interfering responses through the selective use of punishment. This procedure may be relatively crude (e.g., giving a piece of sugar for the right response) or relatively sophisticated in terms of the frequency, timing, and nature of the reward.

In the practice of behavior therapy all these principles may become more complex in application than they appear in theory. In addition, the patient's history and the nature of the difficulties must be assessed to determine the proper strategy or set of strategies to be employed. But although the list of more specialized approaches (such as imparting rational beliefs, the stopping of thought, emotional flooding, and group desensitization) continue to grow, they do not constitute new principles but rather specialized applications of those already discussed.

Applications

A major application of resocializing principles to learning is the teaching machine that presents discrete units of information with immediate objective feedback. If the student gives the correct response, he is immediately rewarded by being so informed. The use of such individualized instruction procedures has received such widespread attention that it need not be pursued here. Suffice it to say that in principle the approach is sound and that it has on occasion been demonstrated to be strikingly effective. However, the difficulties in writing programs for the machines has often been underestimated. Teachers may be threatened by the automation of what they conceive to be a vital aspect of their function. Parents and legislators are intimidated by its initial expense. However, there can be little doubt that educational technology of this sort will continue to spread as its usefulness is demonstrated, the need increases, and the function of education is redefined.

The classroom can be compared to a Skinner box in which rats are trained. The analogy may not be flattering, but some points of resemblance are clear. When we observe the verbal actions of the teacher as he rewards certain behaviors with a smile, a touch, a privilege or punishes others with a frown, a reprimand, a physical action, we are witnessing the application of behavior therapy techniques. Unfortunately, these actions are not always consistent nor are they necessarily sufficient to reinforce the desired behavior. This is the result because the teacher follows no clearly articulated plan in the application of reward and punishment. Consistency is essential. Although it may do no harm if reward or punishment does not always occur in relation to a given behavior, it is unfortunate if reward and punishment occur for the same behavior. If disrespect for authority is sometimes punished and occasionally rewarded through tolerance, the result is to exaggerate the conflict in the student's mind while doing nothing to eradicate the behavior.

A teacher who praises and blames the student for what seems to be the same action creates only difficulty and frustration. Thus, if she encourages creativity and then penalizes its emergence, the student is worse off than if his creativity had not been encouraged in the first place. It is difficult to be rational about these matters because all people are inconsistent in varying degrees. However, many student problems may be produced as much by inconsistent teacher behavior as from precisely what he rewards or punishes. The behavior therapist is acutely conscious of the example he must set and the impact of his actions on the patient with whom he is working. The teacher is functioning in a more complex situation in which he must be responsible for course content as well as the learning environment in which subject matter is presented. Until the learning environment is more consciously formulated, the simple principles of learning that have been described cannot be effectively applied, to say nothing of the more sophisticated schedules of reinforcement under development.

Because of the specificity of the objectives of most conditioning procedures, they can easily lend themselves to tl e cultivation of a variety of behaviors defined as useful by educators. These might include the development of good study habits, healthy social relations, and realistically high levels of aspiration.

Of course the most effective process of all is to reward or punish in relation to each unit of learning, which is precisely what teaching-machine programs are designed to do, although the reward they offer is only the knowledge that one has made a correct response.

For any more systematic utilization of reward and punishment schedules in the classroom, the teacher needs to be more conscious of the alternatives available. Some of these are traditional aspects of the teaching situation such as marks, disciplinary actions, granting special privileges, and the like. Others that are usually ignored but might be applied include the use of immediate physical gratification such as food, intensive emotional support from the whole class, allowing students greater control over the teaching process as a reward for successful performance, and so on. The problem is more one of reward than punishment because students traditionally look on teachers as persons who make them do things that they would generally prefer not to do, such as sitting still for long periods, listening to endless words, or performing assignments following rules that are uninteresting, unclear, or irrelevant.

Education is not generally viewed as fun, though there are of course notable exceptions. One difference in such instances is in the kinds of rewards offered. To some extent they may consist of immediate sources of gratification, such as praise, involvement, or individualization of instruction. There is in addition a special quality to the rewards that are used; namely, they tend to become stronger as they are applied. For example, if a student is encouraged to develop his natural curiosity through praising him directly, making resources available to him, and demonstrating continuous interest in what he is doing, the action of being curious will manifest itself more freely. Since it is intrinsically satisfying to explore that which one is curious about, the more one is encouraged to do so, the more one will do it and the more rewarded one will be. Later the reward associated with the fulfillment of curiosity will itself be enough to perpetuate the activity without the use of so many external rewards. Such a progression from external imposition to internal application is an essential ingredient of any effective socialization process.

A Class in Conditioning

The most striking statement of the use of systematic conditioning procedures as the basis of the development of human potential is contained in B. F. Skinner's utopian novel, *Walden Two*.[1] However, one need not be willing to redefine society in order to employ conditioning approaches for individual development.

A class on resocialization can pursue a number of alternative paths. Students can be taught to use a conditioning routine such as psychocybernetics for producing changes that would be useful to them.[2] One can employ behavior therapy in its various forms in the classroom in a group situation, using problems that the individual brings up in the group as the focus of the conditioning effort. Both the teacher and other students help apply the appropriate procedures to the individual presenting the problem, so as to understand behavior therapy from the viewpoint of the practitioner. The experience can be enriched by a study of some of the varied literature in this area. The prevailing simplicity of behavior therapies can enable students to study and experiment with them with relative ease. This is valuable not only because of the usefulness of the methods themselves, but also because it provides them with an illustration of the application of scientific findings to the systematic alteration of human behavior.

CHAPTER FIFTEEN

ENVIRONMENTAL
REORGANIZATION

AN aspect of human behavior that is receiving increasing attention from architects, social scientists, information theorists, and other specialists involves the alteration of
the environment within which the student exists. This reorganization concerns three distinct levels: (1) the relation between the student and the material he is studying, (2) the
physical surroundings in which the learning takes place, (3)
the social structure within which education is applied. The
ability to institute planned change on all three levels is a pe-
culiarly human function.

On the first level the application of psychological learning theory and the utilization of computer-oriented information theory have led to a systems approach to individualized
instruction, a concept that may seem to be a contradiction in
terms. It is, however, difficult to have individualized instruction on a large scale without developing a comprehensive
system that is large enough and flexible enough to handle a
variety of different individual responses simultaneously or in
any desired sequence. There is a large literature on individualized instruction and a variety of programs and hardware

developed for its implementation. The possibilities are vast even if the realities are sobering.

Closely related to automated instruction is the use of computer-based simulation gaming in the analysis and control of complex systems. A computer simulation game represents an analytic model of a real series of interrelated events. It is a game because the moves and effects are imaginary, but the process of the game is intended to be an accurate replica of some of the more abstract aspects of the reality that is represented. A good illustration is the simulation of a military battle. The basic moves may involve the manipulation of large numbers of men and material, producing simulated death, widespread destruction, and eventual victory or defeat. The results should parallel those that are to be expected if such moves were made in reality, though no one is hurt in the process.

The advantage of a simulation approach is obvious if the simulation produces results similar to those that might be created in the parallel real situations. It has already been widely applied in a variety of educational, industrial, military, and political situations. Nevertheless, it has made only a small impact on the educational establishment.

In the school setting a computer simulation game is still a special event, one that may be viewed as interesting by the students but which may be viewed with suspicion by educators to whom it seems complex, expensive, and too much fun to be truly educational. It shares with automated instruction the need for specialized instructions and equipment and relies on technological sophistication for proper design. It allows students to move into areas of action previously unreal and inaccessible to them. Although its potential field of application is vast, it is particularly suited to the area of environmental reorganization that has as its essential characteristic the need to alter complex interlocking systems without ever being able to fully predict the precise outcome to be expected.

Social restructuring of the environment, the second level, can take place independently of physical alteration, the third level, but they often occur together. The free university movement is an interesting example of a new form of education based on the needs and interests of students. However, it is essentially a social rather than an architectural innovation. The use of alternate patterns of work and study, such as the program originated at Antioch College, involves both social and physical restructuring.

Attempts at redefining the surroundings for purposes of learning are not unique to the school. Several forms of psychotherapy are based on reorganizing facets of the individual's life space as a means of promoting personal growth. For example, many types of family therapy are based on the assumption that one cannot affect one member of a social system without influencing others. For this reason the entire family is brought into therapy either one at a time or all together in an attempt to change the total situation within which any given family member functions. The focus of these sessions is less upon any one individual than upon the problems that exist between members of the family constellation.

Therapeutic communities are clear examples of an attempt to reorganize a living environment to facilitate treatment. Patients exert considerable influence on the organization of the community and responsibility for its functioning, although the ultimate responsibility is clearly in medical hands. The basic assumption is that all aspects of the community must be related to the therapeutic task. This rarely occurs in most institutional arrangements. In the typical mental hospital the patient must strip himself of his ordinary sources of identification and become a docile inmate. This is useful in terms of running a quiet, well-ordered institution, but it may not facilitate the patient's recovery by developing some sense of autonomy and responsibility which he must have in order to function in the outside community. An analogy exists between such institutions and many school situations. When he enters the building, the student becomes an occupant of a given seat in a classroom and must perform assigned tasks on command, regardless of whether they seem meaningful to him. The effect, if it does not breed rebellion, is similar to that on the mental patient.

More recently a variety of intentional communities and communes have spread across the United States. Whatever their differences in design, they represent attempts of young people to redesign their environment into a simpler and more congenial form. A similar tendency is seen in the free university movement, which with a minimum of external support offers individuals the chance to teach, and others to take, a variety of courses not usually offered in colleges. Such universities may not represent a direct answer to the inadequacy of current curriculums, but like third political parties in the United States, they may lead to reform in the establishment without themselves coming into power.

A striking example of the redesign of environmental conditions for personal exploration and development is found in growth centers currently operating across the United States. Inspired by the Esalen Institute at Big Sur, California, these centers have proliferated. Esalen is a prime example of the use of natural surroundings to create useful conditions for personal work. It is located in the Big Sur region, a remarkable geographic area, where the road hugs the cliff and the mountains drop off suddenly into the Pacific Ocean. Hot sulphur springs come out of the mountainside. The living facilities are adequate but rugged. There are no luxuries such as one might find at a resort, except for a swimming pool that does not receive much use. Nearby is a primeval redwood forest and a winding mountain stream. These features make for an isolated, natural, and dramatic setting that predisposes the individual for unusual events.

A Class in
Environmental Reorganization

It is difficult to separate a class on restructuring the environment from more limited applications. Therefore they will be considered together.

In most instances environmental factors are under control of teachers, administrators, and governing boards. In the classroom there may be limited areas in which the student is free to restructure the setting, such as a bulletin board. Unfortunately such opportunities are usually reserved for the youngest students. One reason for educational apathy is that students feel they have no influence on their surroundings. They participate neither in the teaching process nor in the design of the setting in which it occurs. Yet they have unique resources to bring to bear on such an assignment. They know at first hand how the environment functions because it is a part of their daily life. In this sense the school can be viewed as a workshop in which students learn about society. By aiding in the design and functioning of the school they can learn about other areas of social life. Most educational settings are run like institutional mazes. The student does not design the maze: He seeks to find his way through it successfully. This may be good training for rodents, but it limits the human students to a minimal role in understanding and learning to control the significant aspects of his educational life.

Perhaps the greatest obstacle to overcome before students can be involved in environmental reorganization is the distrust that most teachers and administrators have of students' motivation. They suspect that if the students are not told what to do and carefully supervised, either they will do nothing or that they will get into mischief. There may be some justification for these beliefs, but if this is so it is an outcome of the kind of training experiences through which students are traditionally led. Naturally, they cannot suddenly accept responsibility if they have not learned to manage it previously. Rather than accept this as a self-fulfilling prophecy, a transitional period may be necessary before more student participation in environmental design becomes realistic. If it is a desirable goal, it should be sought.

The notion of asking students how schools should be designed is inherently revolutionary. They may choose to overturn sacred relics of the past, not necessarily out of resentment but possibly because the relics are useless. Much of the student revolt in the colleges is directed toward this aim —giving the students a greater measure of control over their immediate environment. This is a natural response from any growing young adult. As in most forms of social change, the sources of resistance are those who have vested interests. Persons who currently hold the power do not wish to surrender it. This also is natural, but simply because it has been that way in the past and tends through inertia to be projected into the future does not mean it must be accepted.

The ideal of self-determination, the right of the individual significantly to affect his surroundings has been eroded in modern society, but that does not make it less valuable or important. If anything, there is a greater necessity now for such training than in pioneer days when new environments were always available for the strong and resourceful. If the school is an institution that is intended to produce self-reliant citizens, it must emphasize experience to foster such behavior. One of the most natural ways to do this is to involve the students in the design and functioning of the setting in which they spend the major part of the daylight hours.

There are, of course, various institutions in schools intended to achieve such ends—student government, extracurricular clubs, and the like. These are useful, but they do not lead to a significant reorganization of the environment.

It is difficult suddenly to give the students authority. The school is already there so that they cannot influence its physical and architectural form. Despite recent interest in the design of school buildings and the suggestion of original and captivating solutions, few architects have seriously consulted with students in relation to their needs and conceptions. If they did, there might be fewer monuments to architectural originality that failed to serve the living situation. However, it would not be difficult to give students a particular classroom on which to work. Starting from this base, the student can learn about the problems that are involved in environmental reorganization, the kinds of responsibilities they must be willing to accept, and the advantages of proceeding in this way. If they are successful, the process can be extended.

From the point of view of a projected class in environmental reorganization all these aspects can be grouped together within one general issue: How can the living environment be reorganized to maximize student growth? There are two aspects of this issue. First, what can be learned about improving the environment from such academic disciplines as sociology, fine arts, architecture, ecology? Second, how can these findings and experiences be applied by the class to their own situation? Can new patterns of physical and social classroom organization be developed and tested? Can the arts be employed not only to beautify the setting but to inform it and heighten the awareness of students of the goals they have set for themselves?

Environmental reorganization is primarily a function of design. As was so clearly shown in the history of the Bauhaus in pre-war Germany, design can enter any avenue of human expression—art, science, industry, and human relations. A human being is not an isolated phenomenon, no matter how well his power of attention may be developed. Therefore, a heightened sensitivity to the impact of the surroundings that influence him and the opportunity to study and modify them is an important part of any education system that has individual development as its cornerstone.

The basic purpose of such a class might be to redesign the school. This would refer not only to large scale issues such as administrative systems of control, subject matter, and teacher responsibilities but to architectural issues such as selection of building materials and the relation of work spaces to patterns of use. The purpose would be to aid the students to evaluate every aspect of their environment. Whether or not a given solution proved effective would be less important than the awareness of the implicit challenge that might be generated. This class would form a natural complement to others that are focused on the individual and would generate motivation to study more traditional subjects such as art, science, and social science.

CHAPTER SIXTEEN

THE INTEGRATION OF
HUMAN FUNCTIONS

ITT is not enough to cultivate human functions in isolation from one another. They must be related both to each other and to a variety of realistic situations if they are to fulfill their intended purpose. This could be done in a class that had two major foci. The first involves studying the effects of combining methods intended to enhance different functions. For example, students might relate fantasy to movement or sensory awareness to meditation methods. Through a series of such experiments they would discover whether different methods significantly enhanced each other's effectiveness, and if so, for which kinds of experiences. For example, is meditation deepened by sensory awareness questions designed to aid a person become more aware of his own organism?

The second aim would be to teach students how to apply these methods to recurring practical situations with which they are confronted. For example, the student might be faced with an aggressive or threatening person. He would then be asked to apply what he had learned in meditation or body movement or creative behavior classes to the situation. He might attempt to control his thoughts while dealing with an imminent attack; or he might use sensory awareness to focus on the shifting physical reactions produced in him by the situation and avoid being swept up in any automatic response. In this manner the class could act as a laboratory for testing the effectiveness of alternate approaches.

A number of recurrent problems could be utilized. These might include overcoming inner resistance to accomplishing a selected goal, generating energy when needed, increasing sensitivity to an interpersonal event, and improvising an immediate response to emergency situations. If the student practices meeting each of these situations by employing approaches already learned, he will be prepared for them when they occur under normal circumstances. Even more important, he will learn how to apply the specific skills he has learned to the real problems that confront him. From this viewpoint the ordinary school program would become a laboratory for the student in the utilization of his own organism in the terms developed by the Internal Curriculum. The record of his experience could be kept in a daily log and discussed in the class in order to learn how to approach such efforts more effectively. The advantage of working in conjunction with others in such a venture is enormous. Under ordinary conditions, the individual is submerged in events he cannot control and finds it difficult to anticipate. In a class based on critical incidents culled from the daily school program, all activities are viewed as potential growth experience to be subjected to continuous analysis by all students whose individual efforts reinforce each other.

Because of the experimental state of many human potential methods, a further activity needs to be introduced into the school experience to aid in the integration of human functions: the micro-experiment. In this experiment a specific training technique is introduced into a given activity and feedback is immediately obtained from participants on an appropriate data collection device. For example, in one such experiment a student might focus his attention on his breathing as a means of reducing nervousness produced by an imminent final examination. The training method is appropriate to the problem and can be introduced unobtrusively into the situation. After a few minutes of focused attention, the student is asked to describe any physiological or emotional changes that occurred. This information is compared with data obtained from other students taking the examination who did not make this particular effort. Such an experiment is not scientifically elegant, but it does generate useful data on an issue of interest to the students. If the results are sufficiently intriguing, further data can be collected under more controlled conditions.

While the micro-experiment is introduced into the curriculum as a necessary evaluation tool, it offers a number of educational advantages. First, it aids the student in appreciating the usefulness of a scientific orientation to problem-solving. Second, it emphasizes the tentativeness of our current understanding of the methods with which he is working, thus, training him to be realistic in his subjective evaluations of his educational experience. Third, and perhaps most important, it turns the educational experience from a complex routine into a continuing investigation on the frontiers of human experience in which students and teachers are pooling their unique efforts toward common achievement. In this manner, the total program is turned into an experiment and the school is transformed from a demonstration into an evolving organism in which human potential is both the process and the goal.

CHAPTER SEVENTEEN

STRUCTURAL IMPLICATIONS OF THE INTERNAL CURRICULUM

THE preceding discussion of the internal curriculum should raise a number of questions in the reader's mind. For example, when and how do students learn anything in the traditional sense? For what age range is this curriculum designed? What kind of student will it produce? What impact would such a curriculum have on the school that applied it? What long-range impact might it have on the definition of the educational process?

These questions cannot be completely answered. Since the internal curriculum as a whole has not been tried as a complete sequence, there is no way to anticipate its effects. Obviously, one cannot introduce fifteen new courses without eliminating some that are already there, but this is a question of redefinition, not of substitution.

The present curriculum is based on the model of student as rebellious computer into which suitable information must be fed and for which appropriate programming must be developed. This model cannot be applied to the students in the program proposed here. Students studying an internal curriculum will tend to be inner-directed; they will come in contact

120

with their own experience and develop their goals and outer actions from a sense of themselves. What they require is opportunity and access. Individualized instruction techniques may help provide this, because the motivation and skill level of such students may be greater than for students in traditional programs. Such students' utilization of individualized instruction may be more efficient and intense, thus a problem may be in supplying sufficient material to keep them busy. Traditional education is often such a deadening experience that we have little opportunity to observe people who really want to learn about subjects of interest to them. Students often waste large amounts of time in emotional concerns, empty social ritual, and generalized rebellion against authority. If they put that time to productive use, the results could be startling.

Given the opportunity and a proper environment, students want to learn. Curiosity is a basic human trait. It is a bleak testimony to modern civilization that the average student has been so effectively deconditioned in this respect, except in relation to socially disapproved acts such as experimenting with drugs. There, unfortunately, he has maintained his native curiosity.

In his book, *Education and Ecstasy*, George Leonard describes the education of the future as an integration of technology and self-fulfillment, multimedia instruction with a personal growth environment.[1] It is a natural partnership. In such a setting the instructor becomes a guide, a source of experience, inspiration, and critical evaluation. His function as transmitter of information is exchanged for one of human example. This is the key to the kind of alteration in teacher training necessary for the internal curriculum. As part of his training the teacher must be exposed to such a curriculum to help him understand the principles involved. This does not mean that the teacher need not develop a particular area of competence. But this could be simplified and extended by other modes of information transmission such as automated instruction.

Automated instruction is a useful approach to the acquisition of fundamentals. The more advanced aspects of any field will always require direct human contact and exposition, but this will tend more in the direction of tutoring, shared work projects, an apprentice system for promising students, and the like.

Some professional educators might view such an alteration in the teacher's function with alarm. Surrounded as he is by externally imposed requirements for the attainment of degrees and certificates, specified content to be covered at each age level, and national norms of proficiency, he appears to be tied to a system that emphasizes routine and normative standards of group performance. This may be more apparent than real. If the system is a Frankenstein monster, who created it? The educator. He can undo it and put it to rest if he is so inclined.

How this may be approached in elementary and high school is suggested in Part III (p. 147ff.). At the college level the situation is somewhat different. In the typical liberal arts program, the B.A. degree does not really prepare the student for any particular job. Only the professional degrees such as teaching do, and even here further specialized work is usually required. The organization of colleges into fields of concentration is an administrative convenience, an academic tradition, and a method of maintaining the status quo. It is not necessary. In place of chemistry or English, music or history, the student might major in himself. This is the basic principle of the internal curriculum—an orderly progression of techniques and approaches that draws on many fields and a variety of different experiences.

Given the opportunity, students might well swarm to such a personal growth program since they are intrinsically interested in themselves and their own functioning. Many other subjects can be related to this frame of reference and in the process take on a different quality.

It is possible to visualize an internal curriculum within the existing educational framework as a field of concentration and, even more fundamentally, as a force in the redesign of the educational experience in which the role of the teacher and the nature of his training are redefined. This possibility is analytically approached in the following section in an effort to establish a more systematic and scientific basis for the curriculum.

PART II | *Strategies for Changing Behavior*

IN THE previous section we related methods for changing behavior to particular human functions. This approach may mask the fact that these methods, regardless of their focus, are usually complex procedures. Any method for promoting growth and development is usually more subtle than we suspect. Its subtlety becomes evident when it is necessary to provide precise descriptions of the method for purposes of research replication or the training of practitioners. It is further emphasized by recent attempts to simulate complex social processes. Any such effort to synthesize human behavior from its elements quickly reveals the range and complexity of the variables whose nature and temporal relationship must be specified.

If it is true that such methods are in fact sophisticated arrangements of small units of interaction, then traditional approaches to research, training, and application in this area may have been naive. We cannot meaningfully study or apply a process that has many unspecified and uncontrolled elements. The best we can hope for is to establish whether all these elements working together produce a detectable effect, but this demonstration reveals little about why the effect was produced.

To carry the analysis further, we must gain control over relevant variables or redefine the situation to focus in greater detail on component parts. It is ordinarily impossible to gain control over all relevant aspects of a complex social interaction, particularly when the added behavior change is desired. However, it is possible to analyze the component strategies that collectively describe the social interchange if they are studied under conditions independent of the process in which they were first identified. Until such identification has been made, we cannot describe any social process in an economical way. We can only report transcripts of everything that happened, a summary of such happenings as in a clinical record, or make broad generalizations that characterize certain key features of an approach but may ignore other crucial aspects that are often of strategic importance.

All methods for fostering personal growth are embedded in their own social, political, and historical tradition. For purposes of evaluating effects, it is difficult to distinguish between the impact of a method, the circumstances in which it is applied, by whom it is applied, the state of readiness and degree of faith of the subjects, and so on. An advantage of studying components rather than whole methods is that the components can be removed from the unique situation in which they are utilized and studied under other circumstances in which these other kinds of influences can be controlled or systematically varied. This is useful not only from a research viewpoint but also as a means of understanding the process of behavior change itself.

From this orientation the analysis of a variety of methods provides the raw material from which strategies widely employed in a number of different methods can be identified. When we have made such identifications, the prevalence of these strategies in other methods can be examined. Such a comparative analysis should help to cut through the maze of contradictory claims and irrelevant comparisons that are often made for different methods. It is almost impossible to compare two methods with each other. If X and Y cannot be precisely described, then a comparison between them is unlikely to be enlightening. On the other hand, if a specific strategy within X is identified, it is possible to determine whether this strategy is employed in method Y also. For example, the strategy of free association in psychoanalysis, used therapeutically with neurotic individuals, can also be found in Synectics, a method of fostering creative problem-solving among normal persons, although the two methods are otherwise quite different.

The importance of any strategy can be tested by a content analysis that measures how often it is utilized in a variety of different behavior change methods. Other things being equal, it is reasonable to assume that the more widely a strategy is employed, the more powerful it must be. If the methods from which the strategies are drawn have been independently devised by practitioners ignorant of each other's existence, or working toward different goals, in different countries and during different historical periods, the evidence becomes even more impressive. If, for example, an approach to the control of breathing was devised in India 1500 years ago and is rediscovered in Germany in the nineteenth century by someone ignorant of Eastern literature, the recurrence of the same approach is given greater weight.

We are not suggesting that the wide utilization of a particular strategy proves its effectiveness. That issue can be resolved only through direct research. However, lacking such research efforts (and they are now almost nonexistent) a comparative analysis of recurrent strategies could provide a useful approach to estimating the relative importance of different alternatives, assuming that the judgment of the practitioners has some validity and that the continuing utilization of the methods themselves suggests that they have some degree of effectiveness.

In addition to the contribution such an analysis could make to our understanding, it might also help to clarify the training process required for the utilization of these methods. It seems reasonable to assume that if such methods are to be widely employed, they must be simplified to the extent that they can be easily taught and widely utilized in a number of different situations by persons of varying backgrounds.

Component strategies may provide just the proper level for appropriate training efforts. No one would have the temerity to try to teach psychoanalysis in a day. Five years is usually required at most analytic institutes. However, a day is probably sufficient to give an individual a sense of the use of the strategy of "free association." Similarly, years of training may be required adequately to prepare a practitioner in sensory awareness work, but an hour is sufficient to give an individual some sense of how to relax through intensifying his awareness of tension.

There is no effort here to suggest that particular strategies are in any sense equivalent to the complicated procedures from which they are extracted. All that is implied is that important aspects of these procedures may be easily taught, whereas the full process would require much time and special background preparation.

This approach suggests a new means for creating behavior change methods. If one can identify strategies that are widely employed in a variety of different approaches, the strategies could form building blocks for synthesizing new patterns of action that have not yet been developed. Thus, if we conclude that free association and the reinforcement of desired behavior are both useful strategies, we are led to speculate about ways in which these approaches might be combined through the selective reward of open uninhibited behavior. This example is particularly suggestive because it utilizes the approaches of behavior therapies and educational technology on the one hand and the humanistic tradition of insight psychotherapy and affective education on the other. When dealing with component strategies, these theoretical differences become less important. One can reinforce self-actualizing behavior as readily as any other variety of more controlled expression.

In summary, any complex change procedure can be redefined in terms of the component strategies of which it is constituted. These strategies have the advantage of being describable, recurrent in many different methods, and lend themselves to a simplified training process.

The Nature of Component Strategies

We have thus far discussed the implications of component strategies without defining precisely what we mean by this term. We will not attempt to make a formal definition here, but will, rather, emphasize certain criteria that such a strategy should fulfill. First, it should constitute a specific action that is consciously undertaken. Second, it should consist of only one kind of action, not two or three that are amalgamated. Third, it should have as its general objective the improvement of the situation within which it is applied either in terms of task productivity, personal enjoyment, individual growth, or all three.

The significance of these criteria can be judged by applying them. Consider the following example of practitioner behavior:

> The trainer asks the group members to shut their eyes and sense their own breathing. After twenty seconds he says, "Please express out loud any images you see or fantasies that you are having."

There are at least five strategies that are employed in this brief segment of experience.

1. Eliminating a sensory channel of communication (sight).
2. Focusing attention on a physiological rhythm (breathing).
3. Allowing awareness to grow by letting time elapse.
4. Redirecting attention to a different realm of experience (images and fantasies).
5. Asking group members to verbalize private experiences.

Each of these component strategies is a unitary action that could be performed independently in other circumstances. The relation between these components is unknown, i.e., we do not know whether focusing on breathing with eyes open rather than shut would make a great deal of difference or what the effect would be if only five seconds elapsed rather than twenty. These questions may be answered through research, but that is not the immediate issue. Our concern here is to illustrate that even a simple action sequence can be described in terms of component strategies that meet the criteria of our definition.

It should be emphasized that we are not here dealing with a formal system of content analysis that has been carefully standardized for rating reliability. We seek only to demonstrate that components can be isolated and that they do exist in more or less the form that the definition suggests.

When we begin to look at the world from this orientation, rather commonplace events take on an altered significance. For example, a man walks to a street corner, pauses, looks at the red light, hesitates, starts to cross the street at a trot, ignores a disapproving look of an old lady, and walks on. This ordinary event involves a number of strategies. First, when we are uncertain what to do, pause. Second, in uncertain situations search for additional information, i.e., signals. Third, when disobeying customary rules, view the situation as vaguely unpredictable and possibly threatening, and therefore end the situation as quickly as possible. Finally, consciously ignore unsupportive views of one's behavior once action has been taken.

The first impression that one has of this process of redefining social actions into component strategies is that simple things seem to become unnecessarily complex. It may be that the only reason behavioral processes have ever seemed simple is because we have never looked at them closely. As in a decoding problem, certain patterns tend to recur, which begin to lend familiarity to an otherwise foreign set of symbols. If the first step in understanding is the recognition of ignorance, then the sense of bewilderment generated by resolving ordinary activities into microscopic aspects is inevitable. This is true not only of activities that are consciously designed to alter behavior, but any sample of behavior as well, such as crossing the street.

Consider a further example: a student comes to a teacher holding a sheet of paper, and says, "I don't understand this . . . oh, now I see." This event illustrates two important strategies. First, the process of formulating a question in itself helps to obtain an answer. Second, coming to a person who may be in a position to answer the question may help an individual to find the answer for himself. The latter strategy is often applied in psychotherapy.

The pervasiveness of behavioral strategies in life is not surprising. Most social behavior is designed in part to influence other people. As such, it must employ the same kinds of strategies that are consciously utilized by practitioners. It is easier to uncover these strategies by analyzing practitioner techniques than by sifting through records of normal behavior because they are not diluted with the same amount of formalistic redundant behavior that characterizes much social activity. Nevertheless, whether we engage in behavior change activities or simple acts in life, our actions are saturated with these strategies to which we are blind, either because we take them for granted, or are unaware of their existence.

The Training of Practitioners

The traditional training of practitioners combines indoctrination, supervised experience, and the application of a selected set of general principles used with increasing flexibility as the student becomes more experienced. In contrast, an emphasis on component strategies in the training process almost eliminates indoctrination, redefines the meaning of supervision, and provides the trainee with a vast set of specific actions rather than a limited set of global principles. These contrasts are of sufficient importance to deserve some clarification and expansion.

The traditional approach to professional education emphasizes the induction of the student into the professional role to which he aspires. Such a process is clearly useful, but it also blocks future change by limiting the perspective and reducing the originality of the student subjected to it. Thus, most mental health practitioners are trained to rely heavily or almost exclusively on verbal approaches to their clients. They are resistant to adopting the active nonverbal approaches that are characteristic of many of the newer methods in the affective domain.

From the viewpoint of strategic components, this process of indoctrination and careful differentiation of professional roles is largely irrelevant. The practitioner has three essential functions. First, he must diagnose the situation with which he is faced. Second, he must select an appropriate strategy to help rebalance the situation at a more efficient level of functioning. Third, he must apply the strategy. On the face of it, one kind of professional can perform the task as well as another. A social worker and a psychologist, a psychiatrist and a minister all have training that is helpful for performing these tasks. This is not to say that all situations can be handled equally well by anyone. Physiological problems require a medical background, for example. Nonetheless it is much easier to think of training a generalized change agent in this context than in the usual one, which emphasizes the acquisition of complex methods through a master-disciple relationship. Of even greater importance, one can visualize teachers, administrators, and policy makers also adopting such an orientation. Each possesses diagnostic skills and is eminently qualified to act on his decisions. Thus, the component strategy approach is broad enough to constitute a bridge between the specialized and often artificially mysterious world of the mental health practitioners and those whose primary concern is with the education and improvement of the normal segment of the population.

Second, the supervision process is redefined by a focus on component strategies. Under the traditional arrangement, supervision is an extensive and continuous engagement through which some degree of expertise is transferred by comment and exchange focused on case material supplied by the student. Generally the process is most successful when a special quality, orientation, or approach is transferred from the supervisor to the student, broadening the student's intellectual horizons in the process.

In the components approach a broadening function is developed by the study of the strategies themselves because they cut across many different methods and fields. The process of supervising concentrates on three questions. Does the student recognize when diagnostic signs of system imbalance have been given? Does he select the correct strategy to rebalance the system at a greater level of internal efficiency? Does he apply the selected procedure correctly and effectively? The analysis of each of these questions is facilitated by their specific nature and the limited amount of behavior to which they refer. When one looks for system imbalances, one does not look in general terms at a half-hour of interaction. In all likelihood such imbalances occur every minute. When the diagnosis has been made, the selection of appropriate strategies is relatively straightforward. For example, if an individual cannot find the solution to a specific problem, an expressive brainstorming type of strategy may be helpful. If he is tense and worried, a letting-go approach would appear reasonable. If he is disoriented and vague, an attention-directing approach might be useful. As research findings become available, these suggestions can be refined. Instead of recommending a type of strategy, a specific choice may be possible taking into account not only the situation but background characteristics of the subjects.

In relation to the effectiveness with which the beginning practitioner utilizes the strategy, an assessment is not difficult to make. If one is introducing the strategy of testing the limits by forcing an individual to persist in a task until he resolves it, one can check first on whether the individual agrees to the strategy, and second, whether he stays with the defined conditions to the bitter end. The specificity of each stage of the supervision process should enhance its effectiveness and reduce the degree of expertise required of the supervisor.

In contrast to global definitions of how a given kind of practitioner behaves, the student is given a comprehensive but specific set of actions. Ordinarily the practitioner uses such rules as: not making evaluative statements, not attempting to have a positive influence on the individual, not allowing his own biases to unduly influence his actions, receiving payment for professional services, and the like. There is nothing wrong with these principles. They are generalized strategies that are often effective within the context in which most practitioners ordinarily function such as private offices or clinics. However, no strategy is irrevocable. All can and probably should be reversed in certain situations. Thus, for example, it might be helpful in certain instances for the client to pay in terms of what he thinks the service is worth, rather than a previously agreed-to amount. Such a subversive approach would surely shift the nature of practitioner motivation.

The component strategy practitioner is not guided by any set of such relatively absolute guides that tend to rigidify over time, as do all standards of conduct. It is not that such a practitioner has no principles. His basic principles are simple and straightforward—he seeks to improve the level of productivity and satisfaction that characterizes any situation in which he functions and places no particular limit on how this is to be done. The sole exception is that any strategy he utilizes must not produce balance within a given setting at the price of imbalancing it with respect to the larger organizational or institutional context within which it functions. If such should occur, he must redress that balance also.

In summary, it seems clear that the process of training practitioners to utilize a component strategy approach to behavior change is both different from and possibly better than the traditional training approach utilized by practitioners at the present time. Its superiority consists in its being simpler, more direct, more objective, requiring fewer untested assumptions, and being adaptable to a greater variety of persons and purposes.

Having described the general characteristics of the training of component practitioners, it may be helpful to give an example of one way in which such training might take place. In this illustration there are three separate courses that correspond to the three functions of diagnosis, selection of strategy, and application of strategy.

The diagnosis class members meet as a small group, where they interact freely. Whenever a member feels that an imbalance has occurred, he points out its existence and describes the evidence he has observed that has led him to his conclusion.

The following is an imaginary transcript from a small portion of such meeting, beginning with a moment of silence. Persons are indicated by numbers for simplicity. The teacher is No. 1.

(Silence).

4: To me this silence represents evidence that something is not being said that might be said. I am asking myself what I might do to facilitate its emergence.

1: Let's not be concerned with what to do but focus on what is. Are we in an unbalanced situation? If so, what is the evidence?

3: I think so. I observed a lot of nervous moving. 2 is scratching his head nervously. I saw you looking suspiciously at 5. I think a lot is going on here that is not being verbalized.

5: I don't know about any of this, but I do know I am feeling uncomfortable. I wish I were somewhere else.

1: It seems clear that an unbalanced state does exist.

3: Well, one thing that bothers me is that we never seem to get anywhere. I wish we could agree to work together on some task. Is there any reason that we can't? (to 1) Is that against the rules?

1: There are no rules. We are here to interact and diagnose system imbalances.

2: I think if we could just say what we feel, everything would go much easier.

5: So why don't you!

2: If you weren't so self-centered, maybe we could get somewhere.

5: Drop dead!

3: We seem to be entering another imbalanced state, but now things are more out in the open, a personal conflict. I hear it in the words and can see that 2 is getting tense. His fist is clenched. His jaw is tight. And 5 looks angry. His face is red.

1: What about other people who are not directly involved? Does their reaction indicate that they are upset by this threat to the group and the outbreak of hostility . . . ?

In this manner the interaction is analyzed and the evidence for imbalance within the group pointed out.

The second class involves the decision-making process of selecting strategies. Beginning with a discussion of the factors involved in decision making, material is presented to relate available strategies systematically to types of imbalance detected by situational diagnosis. This material forms the basic armament of the practitioner. The following is an imaginary discussion by the instructor of a class that is utilizing the previous transcript from the diagnosis meeting.

INSTRUCTOR: In the transcript from the diagnostic session which you have before you, there are two points at which it would have been appropriate to introduce a strategy. Let's consider each separately. In the first instance there was a silence, owing to a desire to avoid the communication of potentially threatening material that was emerging. What are some possible strategies that might have been employed?

2: How about having everybody write down what they were not expressing but would like to express if it wouldn't be held against them?

3: How about the leader beginning to express some of his own reactions, to set such behavior as a norm?

4: I think an indirect approach would be better. Five minutes of relaxation, and a lot of the apparent tension might evaporate.

6: It seems to me that nonverbal communication would be useful. I would have each person communicate with others without words for five minutes.

INSTRUCTOR: There is a rationale for each of these suggestions. None of them is wrong in an absolute sense. If one feels strongly about a given alternative, that in itself may ensure its partial success. On the other hand they are not equivalent. If one of them takes five minutes from the meeting for a new kind of activity, it interferes with the meeting. This may or may not be an important factor. If one intensifies existing interpersonal conflict, then one has to be prepared to deal with the emergent material. One also has to be clear about the nature of the new equilibrium toward which one is striving. Is one more interested in individual feelings or objective productivity . . . ?

The third class involves the application of the strategy selected by means of a role-playing format. The practitioner is trained to apply any strategy to a given situation that is suggested to him by the instructor or other students. He then receives feedback on his performance from these sources and from a videotape recording, which is available for this purpose. In this manner he learns both how to apply given strategies and maintain behavioral flexibility in shifting from one to the other. The following is an imaginary excerpt from such a training process.

INSTRUCTOR: Here is a small group of individuals with which to work. Your job is to introduce whatever strategy I suggest. We are not concerned with the validity of my choice. That is a different problem. We are concerned with your effectiveness as an applier of a given strategy. Any questions?

TRAINEE: No. How do I begin?

INSTRUCTOR: That is for you to decide. Your first strategy is to enrich the amount of communication that is occurring.

TRAINEE: All right. I would like to begin this meeting by suggesting that we each introduce ourselves to the group by sharing what we consider to be three important things about ourselves.

GROUP MEMBER: Do we have to?

TRAINEE: Is there something you would rather do?

GROUP MEMBER: I don't like to be manipulated.

TRAINEE: Do you feel that I am manipulating you?

GROUP MEMBER: You will if you get the chance.

TRAINEE: Would you mind if we examine a little more your feelings about being manipulated?

GROUP MEMBER: I don't mind.

TRAINEE: How does it feel when you are manipulated? Can you express it as a physical sensation?

GROUP MEMBER: My neck gets tight. It feels like someone is holding my head. I am not permitted to move it the way I want to.

TRAINEE: (taking the group member's head between his hands) Does it feel like this?

GROUP MEMBER: Yes. Damn it! I don't like it.

TRAINEE: Go on. Say how you feel . . . .

Later in the class, after selective video playback, the incident is discussed by the trainee:

TRAINEE: . . . so I had to make a choice, either to ignore him or to deal with him. If I dealt with him, I had to change the strategy I intended to employ and still conform to your instructions. Instead of opening up personal verbal sources of communications, I explored nonverbal concomitants of emotional reactions and utilized that kind of material.

INSTRUCTOR: Yes. That was quite effective. Of course, other group members might have gotten fed up, but you were dealing with an issue of interest to everyone. . . .

There are other alternatives for training practitioners in this approach, but the illustrations are sufficient to suggest the possibilities of such training and to indicate the quality such an approach would have.

The training of change agents must be broadened and simplified if the existing national need is ever to be met. The utilization of a component strategy orientation seems to offer a legitimate approach to this problem. It clarifies the training process, generalizes its effectiveness, and eliminates some of its biases. Further, as scientific findings become available, the basic selection of alternatives will become more objective and effective, which is rarely the case in the current welter of conflicting and untested and largely untestable claims that are made for the popular complex behavior change procedures that surround us today.

The Application of Behavioral Strategies to Educational Settings

A recurrent theme in the previous discussion is that component strategies can be relatively easily applied to a variety of different settings without lengthy specialized training, whereas the methods from which they are extracted cannot.

Assuming that this generalization is correct, how can such application most fruitfully be made in an educational format? The simplest approach is through direct action, i.e., by beginning to introduce strategies within the curriculum and allowing their course to be determined by the effects that are observed and the needs that arise. There are, however, at least four additional approaches that can be envisioned.

The first application is in teacher training. This activity is closely related to practitioner training as discussed in the previous section, but it presents certain unique features. The teacher is not ordinarily viewed as a human relations practitioner but rather as an educational agent of socialization. His efforts are more often normative than innovative. Thus, the utilization of component strategies in teacher training efforts assumes a partial redefinition of the teacher's role—something that is currently occurring in any case, owing to student dissatisfaction, the impact of automation, and the momentum of social change. Within this shifting context, teacher training needs to be redefined to produce teachers of greater behavioral flexibility, who are willing to step outside of traditional boundaries to try new methods and emphasize new approaches. The following extract of an introductory statement by a teacher's college professor to a class of new students is illustrative of the kind of impact the component strategies orientation might have on such an educational process:

> Most of you expect that we will teach you what to do when you are in the classroom. This is of course true. What you may be overlooking is that we also teach you what to ignore. Generally, what most teachers are taught to avoid is of greater significance than what they are taught to do. For example, most teachers are taught to ignore the reaction of the students to what they are saying. Any person who lectures cannot really afford to know what is going on in the audience. If he knew how many were bored, or were thinking about other things, or were observing something about his own behavior that is attractive or distracting, he could never go on. So we are trained to assume that people are interested in what we are doing. Only downright revolt brings us up short. When we begin to doubt student interest, we retreat to morality and social necessity to justify our actions. We say it is good for them, whether they like it or not.
>
> Now here we are going to be working from a very different premise. We suggest that you utilize the material students present to you to carry them to a better place than where they started from. To do this we are going to teach you three kinds of things that were not taught before—first, how to recognize the signs of unrest, dissatisfaction, and disequilibrium within the classroom before they become so blatant as to be unavoidable; second, a series of actions you can take to utilize these imbalances constructively; and third, training in the application of these actions, which we will call component strategies.

A second area of application is in the teaching of subject matter. Although the utilization of strategies in ordinary teaching should be developed by joint efforts between change practitioners and teachers, an example can be given to illustrate the kind of possibility that is envisioned for the application of several different strategies in the learning process.

TEACHER: In the next period we will be working on arithmetic. Those of you who wish, can continue with your teaching machine programs. Those of you who have special projects can use the time to work on them. In the class itself we shall be examining why we are studying arithmetic and how it will be applied in situations we will need to face later on. (Class divides into different activities.)

TEACHER: Now, those of you who are still here don't have a special project and don't want to work on the machine. Why not? Let us just take a minute to express some of your feelings about math. (*Verbalizing emotional reactions*)

STUDENT: Math bores me.

STUDENT: I am no good at it.

STUDENT: I think the machine is stupid.

TEACHER: I am going to ask you now to draw a picture that expresses how you feel about mathematics. (*Concretizing emotional states*) Now let us put these pictures on the bulletin board.

For the next fifteen minutes different children explain what their pictures are intended to represent. (*Translating*)

TEACHER: Now, I want you to think of different situations in which you might need to know something about arithmetic. Just call them out. (*Enhancing motivation through visualization*)

STUDENT: Making change.

STUDENT: Reading something about science.

STUDENT: Counting your allowance to see if your parents made a mistake.

STUDENT: Investing in the stock market.

TEACHER: Let's look at some of these situations in more detail and see what you actually are going to have to understand. . . .

A third area of more specialized interest is the development of an automated approach to affective education. Interest in programmed learning provides a vehicle for such an extension of educational horizons. The major danger in these efforts to introduce computerized education is that it can turn into a regimenting rather than a liberating influence. Teachers can be freed for more creative activities, or they can be eliminated by automation in the interests of economy. The utilization of affective methods in such a development can help to swing the balance in the former direction.

Affective strategies lend themselves to automation in the sense that they can be precisely described and classified in terms of their effects. When stored in a computer with subsidiary information that is known about them, such as influence of subject characteristics, group variables, and environmental setting, the strategies are available as needed to meet a given situation in or out of the classroom. Such a facility could be accessible to students and teachers alike through equipment for man-machine communications.

A fourth and closely related application is the utilization of such strategies to improve professional and parent-teacher relationships. In principle the problems and opportunities are similar to the student-teacher uses just described, but the social characteristics of the situation are somewhat different.

One can visualize a leader trained to recognize system imbalance chairing a staff meeting. The following extract is illustrative of how such a meeting might function.

LEADER: We have been discussing several budget items for the last half hour without coming any closer to agreement. Perhaps this is due to the real issues involved, but perhaps not. I would like to take five minutes now to play back an extract of our conversation. I will ask half of you to analyze the content of what is being said. The other half will analyze what is being felt.

(The recording is played back.)

Now will each group meet and prepare a brief verbal report on what you have heard. (They meet for five minutes.)

REPORT 1: In brief, the logic of the argument suggests that everyone favors increasing the first budget item, but no agreement could be reached about it.

REPORT 2: . . . so in summary we detected two subgroups who are antagonistic to one another. They seem to differ in terms of background and experience on this committee. Our feeling was that they would not agree on anything if they could help it.

LEADER: With these points in mind let's resume the meeting. . . .

The existence of a central computer storage unit within the school to aid in the utilization of component strategies offers opportunities not only for application but also for preliminary research. Whenever the computer is utilized to make a recommendation for teacher, student, administrator, it is comparatively easy to describe the apparent outcome for only a moment at the terminal is needed. For example, after the staff meeting just described it is a simple matter for the chairman to type a brief account of what happened and his reaction to it.

This process can be facilitated by the use of a standardized notation. Such a system would include descriptive categories to include the general setting (staff meeting), nature of strategy (identified by number), difficulty of administration (rating scale), degree of success (rating scale), and comments if desired. Such information could be typed directly into the computer by the group leader and any other interested party. It might become routine to feed such information in as it was collected. This arrangement would tap rich continuous sources of data without imposing a burden on anyone, giving all the sense that their experience was not only unique, which in one sense it is, but also a contribution to general understanding.

If one visualizes groups of schools joined in a common computer network, as is often projected in forecasts of the future of education, it is possible to imagine that a great deal of information could be collected about the utilization of strategies in a painless manner. The computer could operate on this information continuously so as to alter the relative positions and priorities attached to different strategies, thus achieving greater precision in describing the relative effectiveness of a given strategy in different kinds of situations. Even though the quality of information provided might be poor in a scientific sense, its cumulative impact could be substantial, just as the opinions of a number of untrained judges may be pooled to achieve satisfactory reliability. Such work would not take the place of more careful research, but it would certainly supplement it and generate many hypotheses which laboratory research could then subject to more careful and crucial testing.

The application of behavioral strategies in education depends ultimately upon the same factors as exist in any other normal social setting: the resistance to change, the willingness to make the effort consciously to diagnose continuing situations, and the redefinition of the key roles of students, teacher and administrator. The need for such application is clear and cannot be avoided. The question is, rather: When such change occurs will it correspond to external demands for some kind of alteration regardless of its merit validity or fundamental character? Or will it be possible to introduce creative innovations that integrate the power of scientific experimentation, a careful redefinition and generalization of the functioning of human relations practitioners, and the possibility of systematic, broad, and cumulative application to a variety of practical situations such as have been described? *

The foregoing represents an attempt to establish a systematic approach to the study, training and application of methods which underlie the Internal Curriculum. Other aspects of the implementation of this curriculum, such as the impact it might have on the school which applies it, are illustrated through the use of the scenario which follows.

* A more extended discussion of the technical aspects of a components approach to the study of behavior change is contained in Appendix One.

PART III | *Scenario:*
A School
for Growth

PROLOGUE

THREE figures are seated in a dimly lighted room. As they talk the room becomes lighter.

NUMBER TWO: Why are we here?

NUMBER ONE: To discuss education.

NUMBER THREE: Who wants to talk about that? Everything has already been said.

NUMBER ONE: Very little has happened.

NUMBER TWO: Why are you here?

NUMBER ONE: Because of the waste of children's lives. Every child grows up in school. He spends ten to twenty years in that environment. He is there when he is most open to new experience and least burdened by the practical responsibilities of existence. And the results are very meager. Something is wrong with the whole operation.

NUMBER TWO: That is easy enough to say. What would you change?

NUMBER ONE: I would emphasize education for growth rather than for knowledge.

NUMBER TWO: Is there a difference? Aren't those just words?

NUMBER ONE: I don't think so. Educating for knowledge involves the transmission and assimilation of facts. Its appropriate model is the computer. Most of our educational operations pursue this course. Educating for growth involves the development of the individual. His capacitites and their integration become the primary focus of the experience.

NUMBER TWO: I have heard all this before. It will not lead anywhere.

NUMBER THREE: Why not?

NUMBER TWO: The forces against change are too great. Perhaps the
present system is wasteful and inefficient. Perhaps the educational equivalent of an ecological disaster is creeping upon us.
But people will not change. The money and the power are in
conservative hands. Sweeping reforms are unlikely. And in
any case, what is there to do; let the students run wild, abolish
classes and work only on special projects? Meet in the community rather than the school? Where would all this lead?

NUMBER ONE: There are other alternatives. Breaking down the system might be a temporary relief, but it would not lead very
far. If there is something fundamentally wrong, it is because
we are ignoring vital areas and using antiquated tools.

NUMBER TWO: When I went to school some years ago, I didn't like
all the teachers, but I certainly learned something. I looked
back on that period in my life very fondly. To have the opportunity to learn is a great luxury. Why is everyone so concerned
with pampering students? It doesn't hurt them to sweat a little.

NUMBER ONE: I didn't say they shouldn't sweat.

NUMBER TWO: Then what is all this conversation about? Why are
we here?

NUMBER ONE: I know why I am here.

NUMBER THREE: Why?

NUMBER ONE: Because there is something I need to say.

NUMBER THREE: I suppose I am here to listen though I don't think
there is anything left to say. This is the latter day of last minute solutions that might have worked twenty years ago but are
ineffective now. Still I might be wrong.

NUMBER TWO: And who am I supposed to represent?

NUMBER ONE: If you don't want to hear me and you have nothing
to say, you must be here to stop me from speaking.

NUMBER TWO: I wish I could. Words are cheap. You may excite a
few emotional busybodies, but that won't have a significant
effect on anything. The system is established and assured.

NUMBER ONE: Then why do I disturb you?

NUMBER TWO: You don't actually. I am here just to keep an eye on
things. We have you under observation.

NUMBER ONE: Who is "we?"

NUMBER TWO: The people who have hired my services. It would be unprofessional to reveal their identity. . . .

NUMBER THREE: What is it you want to say! I can't stay here forever.

NUMBER ONE: It is quite simple. If you think back over the course of your life, you can probably recall instances when your level of functioning was heightened to a significant degree; when your feelings, sensations, endurance, creativity, empathy or religious awareness operated at an unusual level. These are the moments and the experiences that constitute our most precious possessions. They are the necklace of events which we wear in old age: moments in love, in communion, in effortless action, in creative insight, in sudden understanding; moments when life ceases to be routine and reveals itself in shimmering innocence. We usually function at a much lower level. It is the job of education to increase the level of functioning. Everything else is secondary. Education must serve the individual rather than make him its victim.

NUMBER THREE: But is it possible?

NUMBER ONE: Is what possible?

NUMBER THREE: To increase these experiences.

NUMBER ONE: If the desire is great and one is willing to look in strange places, one can discover methods for enhancing any of them. The meaning of education is the development of the individual.

NUMBER THREE: Are you sure that methods exist?

NUMBER ONE: I am sure. There have always been a few men who put their own growth before all else, whether they lived in caves or palaces. They have left us an incalculable heritage. Most of it is not in the classroom. Some of it is not even in our own culture. But the world shrinks. Other cultures become more accessible. We can tap their experiences more easily than before.

NUMBER THREE: Why hasn't it happened?

NUMBER ONE: It is beginning. That is why I am here, to suggest the possibility. You are quiet, sir.

NUMBER TWO: Yes, but I am listening. One question has been running through my mind. Where precisely do you intend to begin this revolution?

NUMBER ONE: You are the last person I would tell.

NUMBER TWO: That is your privilege.

NUMBER ONE: Why are you against the progress of the human spirit?

NUMBER TWO: You don't understand my position. I am a professional. I do not let my own opinions interfere with my functioning. I am here to listen, evaluate, and report. It is for other minds than mine to decide on appropriate action if any need be taken.

NUMBER THREE: I have to go. I have heard enough.

NUMBER ONE: Go, but you have hardly heard anything at all.

NUMBER TWO: It has been a pleasure to meet you both.

NUMBER ONE: Next time why don't "they" come themselves?

NUMBER TWO: They are much too busy.

NUMBER THREE: Doing what? I am pretty busy myself.

NUMBER TWO: Doing the work of the world. I can transmit your invitation to them, but I doubt that it will have any effect. Goodby, gentlemen.

NUMBER ONE: Goodby to you both.

NUMBER THREE: Perhaps we shall meet again.

A DAY AT THE SCHOOL

IF THE Internal Curriculum is made the basis of an educational experience a school for growth will come into existence.

This is a day in the life of such a school.

Morning

It is still early. Formal classes have not begun. Walking through the entrance one is immediately struck by a slowly rotating system of colored lights reflected in a translucent human figure that stands nine feet tall. These shifting colors are coordinated with a series of electronic sounds that seem to be keyed not only to hue of the light but its intensity and saturation as well.

Have they forgotten to turn the mechanism off or does it run perpetually? What is the strange material on the floors? It seems spongy as if it had been spread on with a trowel. I wonder why the building is unlocked? Are there alarms hidden in the walls? I have heard some strange rumors. But at the moment, with the sun streaming in, the school looks attractive and innocent.

What is that odor? It smells like a combination of old leather and pickled beets. Where does it come from? It seems to be changing to pine and salt water. Maybe they program odors like a musical composition. Now I smell peat moss and musk and something else, perhaps orange blossom.

None of the walls looks very solid. I always remember schools built like fortresses. Taxpayers want their money to be visible. These walls look flimsy, more like visual barriers than supports. I wonder what would happen if I pushed one. . . . It moves. It must be on ball bearings. It seems to move any way I want.

There don't seem to be any doors. I guess they just move the walls. What are those strange large free-form shapes? They look too crude to be sculpture. Perhaps they direct and concentrate sound.

There are sections of garden, grass, flowers, and plants. I wonder if those are real birds I hear or just taped sound. No, they are real, near the ceiling under bright lights. There does not seem to be any glass. They must stay where the light is bright. What a lovely idea!

This part of the wall seems to be a translucent screen. There must be several slide projectors on the other side. There certainly are some strange combinations of pictures, Babylonian lions and Picasso's *Guernica*? . . .

The students must take all this for granted. Why shouldn't they? The technology has existed for some time. I doubt that it is very expensive. The school is a heated shell, a soap bubble, real but evanescent. I suppose those large plastic domes let in as much heat as they lose. It is beautiful to be able to look up and see the sky overhead. I don't know why, but there is something comforting about this atmosphere. It has an intense quiet, like a cat that is only lightly asleep. One walks cautiously but with enjoyment.

Should I just wander around like this or wait for someone to come in. Where is the custodial staff? It must be 8:30.

There ought to be some administrators around or at least some secretaries. There is something distinctly odd about the organization of this place. When I wrote that I would be coming, the answer I received was "Come if you want, when you want, but don't expect a reception. We are here. Signed Jennie Williams, student." I was insulted at first, but it made me wonder. Maybe the students decide who comes and who doesn't. Anyway here I am, curious, getting lonely and feeling a little guilty. I am almost tempted to go quietly before anyone knows I was ever here. There was a postscript to that note I got from Jennie Williams. "If you don't find us we'll find you." Well, I can't find them, so I guess I should sit down and wait. I would really like to lie down on the grass but who walks into a strange school and lies down on the floor? Still, what is the harm? The domes seem to be radiating warmth. Perhaps I could stretch out and listen to the water. That is water. I hadn't noticed it before. I don't know how anyone ever learns anything here, when you can lie out under the sun. I suppose it won't matter if I shut my eyes. I woke up very early this morning. I would hear if anyone came. I have this image of little dancing girls floating around me. This is very pleasant. Who cares if anyone ever comes. It was nice of them to build this school just for me. . . .

"Keep your eyes closed. Don't move."
"What!"
"Just stay as you are. You look very peaceful. I am going to work on your head. Your eyes look tired."
"Who are you?"
"Does it matter? Try to experience how you feel and forget about everything else."

(It is a girl or a woman, that much I can tell. Her hands are warm and strong. She must do some manual work. They don't feel like a student's hands. Why is she tapping on my head? It feels like little hailstones. . . . That's better. She stopped. The top of my head is throbbing. . . . Now my face. She seems to know what she is doing. This whole thing is really crazy. We are total strangers.)

"Stop thinking so much. Can't you just accept the experience for what it is and not try to make so much out of it?"

"How do you know what I am thinking?"

"It isn't hard. Every time you start to think, or what you call thinking, your scalp gets tighter or you grimace, or the small muscles in your eyes tremble."

"Can I open my eyes now?"

"How can I stop you? But once you do, the situation will be finished."

"I feel very helpless with my eyes closed."

"Do you object to that?"

"Not really. I am enjoying it. I don't want to open my eyes."

"Then don't. Now I am going to break up some of the tension in your neck. Don't fight me or it will just hurt more."

"Are you a chiropractor?"

"I know what I am doing. There! Was that so bad? Did you hear the cracking?"

"You took me by surprise. Next time I will be waiting and it will hurt."

"Why don't you just pay attention to how it feels right now? Describe it."

"Some of the tension has been broken. I can feel warmth returning. I feel pain, too, but I know it was there all the time. I was numb to it. Wow! You got me again. Just when I had forgotten about you."

"The psychological moment. Now you can open your eyes, if you want to."

"You are only fifteen years old. I thought you were a teacher."

"I do help out in the sensory awareness class and I am sixteen. Does it matter?"

"I suppose not. Thank you. I feel much more relaxed."

"I have to go now. Try to hold on to what you feel. Pay attention to it every once and a while or it will all go away. Goodby."

"Goodby." She walks away quietly.

Is that a teacher coming?

"Excuse me. I am visiting. Is there anywhere I should go to check in."

"No. You are already in."

"But what do I do now that I am here?"

"What do you want to do?"

"How should I know? I just got here."

"Why did you come?"

"I had heard about the school. I am interested in educational innovation.

"What did you come to find out?"

"Is this the way you greet all visitors, put them through an inquisition? I should think you would want to impress me."

"When you walk through the front door of this school, you have to be willing to take responsibility for your own actions. I must get to my class."

"What is it?"

"It wouldn't be appropriate for you. Why don't you wander down the hall? Just go anywhere you want to. The students are used to it."

"What did you say you teach?"

"I don't teach anything. I am a parent. Just make yourself at home."

I watch him walk down the hall, but he doesn't look back. All right. I will do just what he says and look the place over. Now that's strange. That fellow mopping the floor looks more like a student than a janitor.

"Young man. Could I ask you something?"

"My name is Jerry."

"What do you do here?"

"I am mopping the floor."

"What else do you do?"

"Check the furnace. Next week I will be taking out the garbage."

"Next week? Isn't it going to pile up?"

"Somebody else is doing it now."

"You seem rather young for this sort of work. Are you a high school drop-out?"

"Hell no, I am a student."

"You do this work to earn extra money?"

"No, Mister, I do it the same as everyone else. It is part of our work."

"Aren't there any janitors to take care of the building?"

"It is our building. We take care of it."

"You don't get paid?"

"No. I don't get paid. We do everything that has to be done."

"But that is such a waste of time. Shouldn't you be studying?"

"I am studying actually. I am practicing some concentration exercises. Sometimes I do role playing."

"Do the principals and administrators mop the floor, too, or just the students?"

"The who? I told you. This is our school. We do everything. If we run into a problem that we can't handle, then we ask for help."

"Isn't there an administrator or a president?"

"There is and there isn't. Somebody has to sign papers and appear in public for us. But that is only because the world expects it. Here it isn't like that. We are all in it together."

"But how can you say that you are the equal of an adult who has had greater experience than you?"

"I didn't say we were equal. We are all different. In some ways kids are stupid and idealistic."

"You're the first one I ever heard admit it."

"But adults can be awfully frozen. You look a little scared yourself."

"Oh, really? If you run the school, what do the teachers do?"

"We all do it together. Everybody does what is needed and what they need. It doesn't sound very practical when I say it that way, but it really is. We don't even think about it much. How could it be any other way?"

"Don't let me keep you from your work. I'll just walk on down the hall."

"I'm working while we are talking. Every time you use the word "I," I shift my attention to a different part of the body. We follow a regular sequence. Left arm, right arm, left leg, right leg, forehead, throat, chest, solar plexus, pit of stomach, sex organs, and then up the back."

"And you have been doing all that while we talked?"

"Sure. I am still doing it."

"But why?"

"It is part of my homework in 'everyday meditation.' "

"What is the value of it?"

"I am learning to divide my attention. But you might not understand that either. Just say that if we don't bring what we learn into everyday situations, there isn't much point to what we learn, right?"

"How do your parents feel about all this?"

"About what?"

"The school. The strange things you learn."

"They're not so strange. The school is open. If they want to come and watch or participate, they do. There are some problems, but we work them out. I have to go now."

"Goodby."

A strange boy. He seems from a different world. And yet he was quite ordinary, as if he had been practicing his multiplication tables. I don't know why this whole situation is beginning to irritate me. Somebody should be trying to explain things, paying attention to me."

"Hello."

"Hello. Where did you come from?"

"I'm on my way to empathy class. I was experiencing what the wall was feeling when I saw you. I realized that you were lonely and uncomfortable. So here I am."

"You can tell just by looking at me?"

"Of course. Can't you? The thing I can't figure out is how people prevent themselves from seeing."

"You weren't born seeing."

"Really you were. We get it knocked out of us. Or we start getting afraid. Sometimes it is too painful to see. It is a responsibility."

"You mean you might have to go up to strange men and make them feel better. Is that part of empathy class?"

"No. That is just me, but I suppose it is part of 'roles.' "

"What?"

"I mean doing what the situation requires and all that."

"At least they teach you to be polite."

"Are you really as stupid as you pretend?"

"I hope not. Don't they teach you to be polite?"

"No. Of course not. You can't learn how to act out of a book. We learn how to react to the situation. Then you can't go wrong, can you?"

"May I come to empathy class with you?"

"If you like."

"Where is it going to be held?"

"That isn't my job. I was just supposed to find a subject."

"You mean me."

"Yes. I am afraid so. I don't know where the class is going to be held. How can we tell until we see what we need?"

"Don't you have assigned classrooms?"

"What for?"

"So you know where to go."

"No, no. We have our friendly neighborhood computer for all that. Do you want to know how it works?"

"Yes. I would very much like to know."

"Well, the class starts in a neutral area . . . that's a place that has no special quality. There are seven such sites around the building. We call them 'nothing spots.' It has to do with architecture, lines of force. I don't know what all. Anyway, we start from there and get under way. Then when we begin to see what we need for the session we just ask FNC (friendly neighborhood computer) where those resources are available. If they are in use, we make do."

"That sounds inefficient."

"It might be if we had only one of everything. But you have walked around. Most of the things we want we can put together. The specialized equipment is altogether in one place. Most of it is multipurpose. The slide projectors, for example, can project ten separate sequences independently. It is no big deal. So FNC tells us where to go and what is available. And that is where we go. Anyway, here we are at a nothing spot."

"Where is everybody else? I thought this was a class."

"Who knows? Maybe they are at other nothing spots. Maybe they are watching over television."

"Is this place bugged?"

"Of course. Every place in the school is open."

"Big brother is watching."

"Oh boy! You really are something. What is there to hide?"

"So far as I am concerned, quite a lot."

"How are you ever going to learn anything about anything if you take that attitude? We do it because it is the easiest way to be everywhere at once."

"But why?"

"So you can decide where you want to go for one thing. And just to learn and enjoy."

"Maybe you're used to it, but it really bothers me. I don't like the idea of strangers watching me. It is the same feeling I used to get in the subway when the train suddenly stopped between stations and people avoided each other's eyes. No one really wants to look unless he is sure he is safe."

"You remind me of my father. He really hit the ceiling when

he discovered that he was being watched without his permission."
"That's what bothers me. It's an invasion of privacy. I should
think it would be the last thing you kids would want."
"You really don't understand. What is so great about privacy?
There is only one way to have privacy, by controlling your atten-
tion. If you can do that, no one can influence you. If you can't,
then what difference does anything else make? Anyway, whoever
you are . . . you are in a nothing spot. Do you feel the difference?"
"I don't know, I . . ."
"Don't think too much about it. Doesn't it feel different?"
"It is quiet, empty. I don't feel drawn in any particular di-
rection. Am I part of some experiment?"
"At least one, ours."
"Don't you know about others?"
"How can I know? Maybe the ESP class is trying to read your
mind. Maybe the ethics class is diagnosing your value system.
Maybe the role class is improvising a scene with you and your wife.
Are you married?"
"No."
"Well, then, how you would act if you were."
"Look, I came here in good faith. I don't like being used as a
guinea pig. Nobody asked me."
"If I hadn't told you, you would have never known the dif-
ference."
"Is that what they teach you in ethics?"
"Now, don't get so tense about it. We all use each other all the
time. We use everything we can get our hands on. We are here to
learn, aren't we?"
"I suppose I must seem old-fashioned to you."
"Just someone who was mostly created by society. You really
don't have much of a sense of yourself or you wouldn't be worried
about all these things. Anyway, the experiment is over."
"When did it begin and what was it for?"
"It was just an exercise. When a stranger comes along, we all
tune in on him and try to empathize with him. Everybody who is
watching writes down their reactions. Then later in the class we will
compare results and analyze instances where we differ."
"You do this with just anybody?"
"The more variety the better—visitors, delivery boys, parents,
each other. But it is better if the person is a stranger. Then we don't
have direct knowledge to go on. I have to go now for the discussion. See you around."

"Isn't there someone in charge whom I could talk to?"

"You could see 'Wise Owl,' but I think you are better off looking into things for yourself."

"Is Wise Owl a computer?"

"No. She is an old woman who has taught here a long time. Her real name is Norma McNaughton. We call her 'Wise Owl.' "

"What do they call you?"

"Little Bean. I have to go now. See you around. I think we will call you Dumb Head."

"I don't suppose I have any choice."

"You earn your name. You don't select it. Goodby, Dumb Head. Don't look so angry. You don't even know what it means."

"Well, tell me then."

"Everyone's name is a puzzle. Maybe you will have a new name before you leave."

She disappears behind a wall.

(I should have appreciated this place when it was quiet. I feel a little paranoid. I keep looking for microphones.)

"Don't take yourself so seriously, Dumb Head. You aren't all that interesting you know."

"Who said that? I don't see anyone."

"I am the voice of Christmas Past. Ha-ha."

"What in the hell is going on now!"

"Poor old DH. Getting himself in such a stew. If you are going to be so worried about your delicate, precious ego, how are you ever going to see anything?"

"Where are you?"

"We are here at the other end of the room, behind five walls."

"First you are nice to me and then you irritate me. You can drive a rat crazy like that. Are you a bunch of demented kids? Where are the teachers? For Christ's sake, I am your friend. Why don't you treat me like one!"

"Well, you see Mr. DH, we treat everyone the same. We are here to learn."

"Now you sound like a teacher. Why don't you come out where I can see you and we can talk? What kind of class is this anyway?"

"This is an improvisation, actually. When you appeared we decided to work you into it."

"What is the story?"

"Well, you see, this man comes in the school. He looks all right, but actually he is an interplanetary spy and we all have to act very normal, but at the same time we are trying to think what to do. Can you be a spy?"

"I can try, but aren't you all a little old for this? It sounds more like a game for six-year olds."

"We are six-year olds."

"I'm seven."

"And I am one hundred and seventeen. My name is Toddles."

"What am I supposed to do?"

"You could think out loud. Quiet, please. Spy soliloquy."

"I'll try. I am doing pretty well so far. No one suspects anything. No alarm seems to have been activated, but I must be on my guard. This system is full of surprises. I am under constant observation. I must remember to keep to my role—slightly stuffy but a friendly observer who is being put upon. This should make them feel slightly guilty and help them overlook any inconsistencies in my behavior."

"That was quite good. Would you like to join the class?"

"Where are you?"

"Just push the wall on your right."

I push gently and it falls away. There are seven twelve-year olds.

"You aren't six."

"You aren't a spy."

"Where is the teacher?"

"We asked him to leave."

"Are you learning anything without him?"

"We are learning whether we need him or not, and we are learning something about teaching."

"Where is he?"

"I think he is in the catharsis area. Would you like to see him?"

On an adjoining wall a large picture appears of a room with padded floors and walls. There are various objects lying around in various stages of destruction.

"Is that your teacher?"

"Yeah, that's him. The one who is about to scream. Wait till you hear this!"

The man in the picture appears in a frenzy. He jumps up and down, pounds on the floor and suddenly breaks into wild screams. He looks like a complete madman.

"He's quite effective, isn't he?"

"Is that person really your teacher? He should be locked up."

"You would look at it like that, wouldn't you?"

"Well, how do you look at it?"

"We hurt his feelings. He is angry. I feel sorry for him now. Maybe we should ask him to come back."

"I wouldn't be in the same room with him."

"But old Mr. Dumb Head, he was only ventilating his feelings."

"The last person I saw do that was in an insane asylum. How can you take it so calmly?"

"Well, you see Lion Mouth (that's who you are watching) teaches emotional expression. Sometimes he comes on too strong."

"Was he just pretending?"

"No, no. Not at all. What are we going to do with you? You are just so scared about everything. Haven't you ever gotten angry? Haven't you felt like screaming and carrying on?"

"Yes, but I am not crazy enough to do it."

"All right. In the everyday world people wouldn't understand. They expect you to control yourself. If you don't, they feel threatened and put you away. But here it is different. We are learning how to express what we feel and how to make use of it. If you don't express your feelings, you are cutting yourself off from a lot of energy. We need all the force we can get. There is a lot to do. So we don't hold it back. We go to the CR and let loose and then we come back. No one gets hurt. We learn to express difficult or violent reactions, and we learn to control them. You can't control anything if you are scared to experience it. Don't you see?"

"But what good does it do? Every drunk can run wild."

"Here comes Lion Mouth. You can ask him. Hello, LM. This is Dumb Head. He is scared of you."

"Hello. I am Mr. . . . I mean Dumb Head. How are you feeling?"

"Much better, DH. I was just recalling once when my father sent me out of the room. I think he and my mother wanted to go to bed together. Anyway, I was real angry at the time. They sent me out of the room just like you little twirps. Yes, I feel very much better."

"Dumb Head was asking about what good it did to carry on like that."

"Yes, I suppose he would. They didn't give him that name for nothing. But I apologize. You must be having a rough time. When someone comes from a session in the catharsis room, you can't pay too much attention to him for a few minutes. But I'll try to give you an answer, if you haven't figured it out already."

"I can see that ventilating feeling may be useful, particularly if it helps you relive old, unresolved conflicts."

"Yes, there is that aspect, but there are other things. I don't want my mechanism to get fouled up. If I am angry and pretend it isn't so, the garbage has to go somewhere. It builds up. It takes energy to keep it hidden. It is so much simpler and more natural to express it and be free of it."

"But it must be terrifying, particularly at the beginning."

"It can be scary. But it gets much more terrifying not to do it. After a while you get scared not about what people do, but at what they don't do, the things they carry around inside them waiting to explode. When you get free of some of the tension, you can allow yourself to see it in others. That is what is scary, to watch potential murderers smile."

"I suppose so. I keep looking for the structure in this place and things keep happening too fast for me to find it."

"We used to place a good deal of emphasis on structure. It gave us comfort and helped us to keep oriented. But what you call structure is really a process intent on perpetuating itself through the imposition of conformity. It created the illusion of stability much like a human body. But get up close to it and what do you see. Cloven Foot, ask FNC to project a picture of living tissue on the screen."

"What code is that?"

"Just type it in. If FNC can't figure it out, there is someone on duty now to work out the code."

"It isn't necessary to go to all that trouble for me."

"But it is. We must use every means at our disposal. We aren't in love with words anymore. Ah, here it is. It seems to be a tissue culture. Some medical test or other. We could turn up the sound track and find out. But that is not the point. Look at it, Dumb Head. What do you see?"

"Trick photography, I suppose. The action is speeded up."

"Forget the technique. It is only speeded up to demonstrate

the point that what appears fixed is actually in process of continuous, sometimes violent, change. Everything is process. This school is process. It has been created not as a structure but as an organism. It has been created to act as a catalyst for growth. Can you even guess what that means?"

"You don't have to be patronizing. I believe in those things myself."

"Sure you believe in them. Every enlightened person does, until the going gets rough. We believe in physical fitness until we are asked to scale a rock cliff. Then we find excuses. We believe until our bluff is called, until someone does something we don't like or that makes us afraid, or, Mr. Dumb Head, that offends our ego. Then growth becomes ominous and change only a short distance from anarchy."

"What does this have to do with the school?"

"It is an organism and we are its parts. But we in turn, each of us, are organisms of many parts. It is very complicated. I don't even know what I am talking about myself anymore."

"One thing I have wanted to ask. What is this business with names?"

"The reason we use these names is . . . well, what sense do ordinary names make? They are labels. A name says who you might be related to, but it isn't very important. We want to say more than that. So we use names to help people remember who they are. People earn them. This way every time someone uses your name, you get something about yourself pounded into you. The names change, when the people change. That is all there is to it."

"Why do you call me Dumb Head?"

"Why do you think?"

"You must think I am stupid."

"No. That is not the reason."

"Why, then?"

"You have to figure that out for yourself. Ask yourself every once in a while about it. Do you want to try an exercise?"

"All right."

"Then shut your eyes and imagine yourself in a valley surrounded by high mountains. Can you see that?"

"Yes."

"Then imagine yourself shouting as loud as you can, 'Why do they call me Dumb Head?' After you do that listen to the echo as it reverberates through the mountain range. That is all. Try it." . . .

"Now what do I do?"

"Nothing. Wait. Later in the day you can try it again."

"How can I get an answer if all I do is ask the question?"

"Perhaps you know the answer already. This is a way for you to allow the truth to emerge. What have you seen so far today?"

"I haven't seen very much. I have talked to some people and have been with this group. That is all."

"What would you like to do now?"

"Part of me wants to see a little of everything. I feel that is what I ought to do."

"What do you want to do?"

"Say the hell with it and take it as it comes."

"Why don't you?"

"As I say. I have a certain responsibility. I have to be able to describe what I see here today to other people. I can't just forget that."

"You have a conflict."

"Yes."

"What are you going to do about it, follow your conscience or follow your impulse?"

"I could go either way."

"But which is right?"

"Is this a class in ethics?"

"No, but we can use it as an illustration. How are you going to decide which is right?"

"I really and truly don't know. The simplest thing would be to deny myself. No one out there would criticize that. But I am not sure."

"What would you suggest, class?"

"Don't get patronizing with us or we will kick you out again, LM."

"How about some role playing?"

"How about a bit of Top Dog/Under Dog Gestalt therapy?"

"Maybe creative problem-solving?"

"Who said Gestalt? Was that you, Slither Brain?"

"Yes."

"Do you want to try that out with DH?"

"Sure. Do you want to do it?"

"I think so, but why do they call you Slither Brain?"

"I have a sneaky mind, what else. Now the idea that I had is

based on the notion that there are two different parts of you in conflict, Top Dog, your superego, as we Freudians might say, and little
old Under Dog, your weak ego. In order to come to some decision
these two parts have to agree on what to do. Understand?"

"I guess so, but what do I do?"

"You talk to yourself. Over here you are Top Dog. Over there
Under Dog. Go ahead."

"It sounds silly."

"It isn't silly if you get into it. Just start. Be Top Dog first. Tell
Under Dog what it should do."

"Listen here, Under Dog. You are not here to enjoy yourself.
Stop acting in this disgraceful manner. Shape up or ship out. I
sound like a top sergeant."

"Don't comment! Stay in it. Be Under Dog."

"All right. You may be stronger than I am, but you are a bully.
You can make me do what you want, but it is only because I am
afraid of you, not because you are right."

"But I am right. How dare you question my authority? I have
the wisdom of the ages behind me. I have your parents' authority. I
speak for society."

"You are full of shit, if you want to know the truth."

"You forget who you are talking to, little man. You may feel
brave right now, but wait until I get you out of here."

"I am not going to let you threaten me. Stop treating me like
an infant. You are not my mother."

"You have to be taken care of. You can't be trusted to go
down the street by yourself."

"Where did you get that crazy idea? I may not be the most
mature person in the world, but I want to be treated with a little respect."

"You remind me of a Scotty barking at a Saint Bernard."

"Maybe I should have started barking long ago. But how are
we ever going to agree?"

"Very simple. You do what I tell you to do. I don't care what
you think so long as you do what I want."

"You should care what I think. You are a dumb head. Oh, my
God! That's the answer. Thank you, Slither Brain. I think I will
leave now. What time is it anyway?"

"Almost noon."

"How do I get out?"

"Just push the wall."

"Goodby. And thank you."

Afternoon

I am alone again, but I feel more at ease. I suppose these walls that turn into doors make me nervous. If walls began to move, anything can happen.

These kids are very lucky. I wonder if they know it. I wonder what happens to them when they leave for the summer or they graduate. I wonder how they get along with their parents.

This place is more like a magic theater than anything else. But do they learn anything? I don't see anyone studying. Maybe they don't care about knowledge.

"Hello."

"Hello. My name is Dumb Head."

"My name is Little Thunder. You don't look like Dumb Head. I think you should be called Little Father, Dumb Head. Can I do something for you?"

"Yes, you can. Where does the learning take place?"

"All around."

"That's not what I mean. Where do people study subjects, like in a regular school?"

"Oh, that. In the arena. Just down the hall."

"I don't see anything."

"Walk to the end of the hall and push the wall."

"Thank you, Little Thunder."

Down the hall. Push the wall and before me is a large round room. It must be 100 feet in diameter. And just one great dome. It looks like a vision of the total learning environment. What a strange atmosphere. As if five symphony orchestras were rehearsing in the same room. But no one seems distracted. Most of the kids seem to be using earphones. I guess that shuts out the noise. Actually it is strangely quiet. All those images on the walls make it seem eerie. That one seems to be a film on history. It looks like the French Revolution. Maybe it is a dramatization of a novel. And that one is in three dimensions. It seems to be a study of atomic fission. I wonder what is on the sound track.

And then that bank of carrels. They seem equipped with screens for movies, tapes, slides. Some of the tables have built-in scientific equipment, sinks, chemicals, microscopes. The thing that interests me is that everyone seems absorbed in what he is doing. No one talks to anyone else.

And there is a set of microfilm readers. I don't see any books. The computer must work with filmed material more easily, and it saves space. I don't see the computer. It must be underground.

This kind of thing must impress visitors—super technology, quiet air of dedication. But it isn't really so much, just a more efficient system of transmitting information. I wish I knew how it worked. I hate to interrupt anyone.

Perhaps this large looseleaf book might tell me something. It seems to be a catalogue, indexed by subject, media, and level of difficulty, with critical comments by students.

I feel like a child with a new toy. But what a fantastic toy, just waiting to be turned on to almost anything I can imagine. And all it needs is this simple numerical code in front of each item. I suppose each machine has its own code. You type in the numbers or speak them into a microphone, or something like that, and it starts. But I wonder. . . ."

"Are you a visitor?"

"Yes."

"Why are you standing there like that with your mouth open?"

"I didn't know I was, but I am puzzled. Could you answer some questions?"

"Surely, Einstein's the name. That's my first name. My last name is Monster. I live here."

"In the school?"

"No, here in the arena and I sleep downstairs with FNC. I take care of it."

"Is this your job or won't they let you out?"

"I don't want to leave. That's why they call me a monster. They make fun of me and say the machine created me. But I don't mind. What would you like to know?"

"Well, I would like to know about you, but before you came up I was wondering how records were kept. Do you use workbooks? Things like that."

"Is that all? It is extremely simple. Every student has a number. All he is to do is sense his number into FNC and it tells him just where he was when he stopped. It keeps records of all tests which he takes. In fact all standard information about the individual is kept there."

"You mean from classes."

"Yes. All around the school at convenient locations there are input controls. Teachers and students routinely feed in quantified reactions of any kind that refer to the individual, regardless of the activity. Each activity has its own code, of course. It may sound complicated, but you get used to it very quickly. These materials are available to the student whenever he needs to consult them."

"Can just anyone look up anyone else?"

"Of course. Are you still hung up on confidentiality?"

"What do you mean, 'still'?"

"We have a storage location on you. I took the liberty of looking at a print-out before I came up to meet you."

"But isn't it dangerous to have this material available to anyone. Can't it be misinterpreted?"

"There are only certain kinds of summary information that can leave this building. The students and staff have agreed on what this should be. It is similar to ordinary school records but more reliable and valid. The rest is for internal consumption."

"Don't you feel worried about other people knowing all about you?"

"It depends. If I assume that we are trying to learn about ourselves and to improve our levels of performance, then the more everyone knows about me the more they can help me. If I assume, however, that others are out to get me, then the less they know the better. I have found the former to be the case."

"How old are you, Einstein Monster?"

"I am ten years old, but I have a high intelligence quotient. I am particularly proficient in Guilford's factors 25, 33, and 116. I am rather a monster, don't you think? I hope that as I grow older that I can allow myself to act in a more childish manner. Right now I find it rather threatening. Are there any other questions?"

"Don't you think you should leave here? Why do they allow you to stay?"

"I want to stay. I enjoy it. I am learning lots of things. I help keep the computer operational. That is socially useful. I know that I will go outside sooner or later. But for now this is my cocoon. I have to go now. I think there may be an information overload in biology. Several students have entered into an informal competition. That sort of thing isn't encouraged, but they do it anyway as a sort of intellectual wrestling match. Goodby, Little Father. Enjoy your stay. Would you like to use any of the mechanisms? Your identification number is 3026."

"Goodby."

I was always interested in celestial mechanics. Let's see if the catalogue recommends anything special. There seem to be a number of courses available but I haven't the time. This item seems to be recommended, "useful and enjoyable but not many facts" Machines 35–40. Let's see if one of them is available. It must be one of these. I suppose you are meant to get into it, this thing that looks like a diving suit. It must be a completely artificial environment, but this suit is too small. There must be a larger one. Over there . . . Now I press these levers protruding from the table with the right numbers and wait.

"Attention. Attention. The following exercises have been found useful in viewing this material: Sensory Awareness 23, Meditation 13, Creativity 63 and Perception 1. If you are not sure of the exercises a summary description can be obtained at this time on request."

Perhaps I should try the first one just to get the idea. I just feed in the numbers.

"Sensory Awareness 23. No outward experience should go unaccompanied by an inner sensation. When perceiving through the senses, always remain aware of what the perception does to your sensations. Does it create warmth, tension, fear, pleasure? A more complete description of this exercise suitable for application by FNC can be found in 625513."

I get the idea. On with the show.

"Please be comfortably seated. You are about to take a simulated space flight which has been programmed to include a visit to various parts of our solar system. Be comfortably seated. If you should become frightened or bored, simply press zero on the console and the simulation will cease."

Oh my God, my seat is slanting backwards. It looks like a countdown.

"All systems go. 10–9–8–7–6–5–4–3–2–ignite."

What are they doing? This tremendous pressure on the whole front of my body. We must be moving. What a strange trembling and the odor of ozone. Is there a short? We must have taken off. All I can see is the sky. What a beautiful effect. The pressure seems to be lessening. If I had known what was coming I would have gone to the bathroom. I wonder how long this is going to take. I'll just watch a few minutes and then stop it.

"Six hours have elapsed since take off. You are heading toward the Moon."

The illusion is remarkable. There is nothing but space and stars and the growing moon. Where did they get these pictures? The astronauts must have taken them. The kids must go out of their minds. But I suppose this is nothing but a simplified simulator. They had those years ago. They trained for flights in them. But this machine can be used for any kind of environment—sound, sight, smell, moving. I know I am sitting in a room. I know that none of this is happening, but I can't believe it. It looks real.

"As we approach the moon you will note that the instrument panel indicates that. . . ."

This must really stimulate motivation to learn astronomy, engineering, geography. I really ought to listen to what the man is saying, but I just want to talk to myself.

". . . down to a depth of 150 feet. The craters that you can see to the right were formed by a process. . . ."

Who wants to memorize isolated abstract facts? It is such an impoverished stupid activity, like using a limousine to pull a tinker toy. Learning for the sake of learning is a perversion. You learn for life, to understand, fulfill, explain what puzzles you. Here and now I am really interested in the moon. I want to know about it. How it was created. What its atmosphere is like, its temperature, its gravity. I have to know if I am going to be on it, walk outside the ship or whatever is going to happen. That must be a key—creating an environment in which the information becomes relevant and applicable. Where am I now? That looks like Mars in the distance. The air smells antiseptic. It is really deathly still. You could go out of your mind in this ship. I can imagine men going mad and stepping out of the airlock to their death, just to get out of this throbbing coffin. It needs a special kind of mentality. I remember once when I was locked in a closet. . . .

"Since the trip to Mars is a lengthy one special preparations, chemical and otherwise will enable you to spend a part of that time in a deep sleep."

. . . What happened? I blacked out. How did they do that? It seemed instantaneous.

"One week has elapsed. You have been asleep. A harmless gas was used. Its effects will wear off momentarily. Please relax and breathe deeply. This material was discovered by Army chemists seeking an antidote for a form of chemical warfare."

I have had enough. I am going to abort. I am not as strong as these kids. I want to get back to reality. THERE! They are all still here. Working away on chemistry, astronomy, history. I am sufficiently impressed. I wish I could stay here a week and just follow my own interests. The only thing that bothers me is that education shouldn't be so interesting. It should be painful. I was hurt. Why should these kids just lap it all up like spring rain?

I am kidding, I suppose. After all, this experiment hasn't been so easy on me. Maybe it isn't on them either.

All this equipment must really cost a fortune. It isn't really economically practical, but it certainly is fascinating. Maybe we could trade in a few atomic bombs to pay for it. But who would want them? There is nothing so worthless as an obsolete weapon system. Maybe some backward country planning a small war.

Let me out of here. I am getting morbid. I guess I can push on any wall.

"Oh, excuse me. I didn't mean to walk right into the middle of your class."
"Just be quiet, please, and stop making all those vibrations."
"I'm sorry. What is this?"
"Not now. Watch if you like. We can talk later. Sit down over there."

Before me sit a group of fifteen crosslegged children, most of them young, with a mixture of older ones. Their eyes are slightly open. They appear to stare at some empty point in space directly in front of their noses. Everyone is silent. They sit with straight backs. It must be some form of meditation. But the children seem so young, eight to ten years old. Perhaps I should imitate them. No. What is the point? I will just wait. That man must be the teacher. What is he doing? Is he going to hit that girl on the back? She doesn't say anything. How long is this going to continue. I feel very conspicuous, but no one is paying attention to me. I think if I screamed, I would be ignored.

"That will be all for today. Come out of it now. Fifteen minutes. No more and no less. Do it intensely, but don't extend it on your own. Goodby, now."

They melt away quietly without talking to each other. There is no point in my asking them anything.

"Well, Little Father, do you have any questions?"
"What was it all about, some form of concentration?"
"This is a class in Introductory Meditation. We were doing Zazen."
"Japanese Buddhism?"
"A Zen exercise. They were counting their breaths and focusing on their center of gravity in the pit of the stomach. They count ten breaths. If they do lose count, they begin again."
"Is that all?"
"It is not so easy. Have you ever tried it?"

"But they are so young. Isn't meditation for late adolescents and adults?"

"So we used to think. Perhaps it has a different quality later on. Right now it is a discipline and a means of harmonizing their experience. I do not know what a Zen monk would think, but we judge by the effect. The children seem to thrive on the discipline. It is an antidote to the vast amount of freedom that surrounds them. So long as they feel that they can control themselves, they can accept the chaos more easily."

"How long does this go on?"

"A year. This is a regular class. They follow a progressive scheme of exercises. By the time they are done they can create a clear inner state at will. A philosopher might say that they can submerge in being. Some go further. We want them to have a fundamental point to which they can refer, a center of their experience. Do you appreciate how important that is?"

"I suppose so."

"You cannot really understand. You lack such a center in yourself."

"I don't know about that."

"Don't be insulted. Very few people have it. It was a familiar idea in the ancient East that the center of a person's experience should be far down in his body. In a physical sense you can appreciate that. An object with a low center of gravity is hard to overturn. If it is curved and is pushed over, it will right itself. But there is more to it than that. Attention is like an object. It will sink if the body is relaxed."

"In our society many people live in their heads. They *are* their thoughts. A small number function from their emotions, in the chest and solar plexus. To do that one must be properly centered. The most powerful energy, the source of life is deep in the trunk. If these children can gain some sense of this experience, it will change the quality of their actions. It opens up a great source of power to them."

"That is what the teacher in emotions said."

"That you need to contact emotions to tap their energy."

"Yes."

"If you were around here long enough, you would hear that thought quite often. That is what this school is really all about, but a lot of visitors go through here and never even suspect it. They go into the arena and are impressed with the technology. Perhaps they take the space ride. That's there more for the visitors than the children. They suggested we put it there at a council meeting last year. Young Warrior made the point that it would be the kind of experience that our parents would approve of, interesting but educational.

"Some people simply go through here and get scared. They leave and make veiled negative comments. Others are intrigued but never return. They would rather have their dream of what we are, then reality. A few would like to move in with the kids, but that is not the point of being a visitor. You should come, absorb, and then leave so as to be able to transmit your impressions. Then some like you discover or are told about energy."

"Why have you told me? I wouldn't have guessed it."

"Various reasons. Einstein Monster told us we should. You seem ready for it. Perhaps the time has come when we want to get a less distorted picture to the outer world. Does it really matter? Would you rather regress to Dumb Head?"

"No. Why is energy so important?"

"This school was created as a place for growth. Nothing grows without energy, lots of energy, from food, air, the sun, other people, and even the cosmos. The reason people rarely grow, other than their lack of motivation, is that they cannot find the quantity and quality of energy that is necessary. Much of it is locked up inside them, or it surrounds them but they do not sense it. Energy flows only in an open system. An electrical engineer understands this. Break the circuit and the current stops. Here we have to reestablish connections and open up new channels in which energy can flow.

"A human being, whether he is little or big, contains a bewildering number of possibilities. But they remain only possibilities unless they are catalyzed and nourished. The mind needs ideas, the heart emotional flow, the body action and sensation, the soul cosmic contact. Each of these things uses different levels of energy. If we can put a child in contact with his diverse energies and teach him how to control them, the rest follows naturally, but it is not easy. I would not have you think that. I did not mean to talk so long. I rarely get to talk about it at all. I hope you have some sense of what I mean."

"I think I do, but I don't want to give you a glib answer. What should I do now?"

"What is different about now?"

"I feel adrift."

"That is because you have no center. Some of your own ideas
are disturbed. Your personality is shaken up. Be thankful. Experience it. Why don't you walk ahead through this wall? There is a
rather restful place to gather your thoughts on the other side. It will
be evening soon."

"Is it that late? I think I will. Perhaps I will see you later."

"Goodby."

Through this wall . . . this is a lovely spot. I always
enjoy the sound of running water. It is soothing, like cold on
a burn.

I am glad I don't have to write a report on this place.
What can you really say about a stream: It flows.

I keep feeling defensive. Something in me wants to tell
them that they are wrong. Maybe they are wrong, but that
isn't the point. I want them to be wrong. Maybe I desperately
want them to be right.

Where is this going to lead? Is it the start of a new age?
Is mankind ready to drop the self-inflicted flirtation with
death that has absorbed its fancy and drunk its blood for
endless centuries? Are these children new seeds on the wind?
I would love to think so. But it may be an illusion. Another
special situation that cannot be repeated . . . dramatic, but
creating more problems than it resolves.

Why am I so concerned? They don't seem to be. Why
must I leave here having made up my mind to damn or to
champion them? They don't need me really. Do I need them?

That thought sends a shiver through me. If I were
younger, or freer, I might come here. But I can't. I shouldn't.
I am here for a day, to visit, to receive, and then to transmit
the atmosphere of the place to others.

Perhaps I should stop thinking. I will try meditating;
putting my attention on my breathing . . . One . . .
Two . . . Three . . . Four . . . Five . . . Why do I think of
myself as a little boy afraid to go in the lunch room? Oh hell,
I lost the count. One . . . Two . . . Three . . . Four . . . Five
. . . I feel better . . . Six . . . Seven . . . Eight . . . the
sound of the water . . . Nine . . . is beautiful . . . Ten . . . I
am relaxing . . . Eleven . . . Oh, hell, I forgot to stop at ten.
How can those little kids get used to this?

It seems much darker outside. . . . The spheres are turning into colored translucent domes. How do they do it? Probably very simple, a few lights and some colored gelatine. Why do they do it? Some budget-minded official ought to protest. Who needs colored lights? It must look beautiful from the outside . . . giant soap bubbles about to float into the sky.

I feel so alone but there is intense activity all around. I must be in the eye of the storm. It is calm.

Energy. Power. It is so objective, dangerous perhaps, but maybe that is my prejudice. When I think of the electricity that flows in my house. It could kill me, but it doesn't. It serves me countless ways so long as I control it. Energy degenerages into orgy and control into authoritarian discipline unless they balance each other. And life without either is a vague pitiful drift.

A visitor to this school should be prepared. But if the experience is the message what can you say except "hang loose."

It is no fun to be broken down. They must pay for what they get.

What is that strange music?

"This is Shelly Agonistes with the late afternoon expression. For this hour I have created an experience with words and light. I suggest that wherever you are, you lie down and look at the sky. My words will be spoken against an automated pattern of lights."

"The day is a necklace of delights.
Each gem is an event drawn from the heart of fire.
The sunrise and the sunset meet in the clasp of darkness
Where they are joined as one. . . ."

I wonder how old he was; probably six and one half. Retarded. He couldn't know what he is talking about . . . could he? Where would that leave me, just beginning, a little farther. Thank God it will soon be night.

Evening

I have been sitting here for a half an hour. Nothing seems to be stirring. I wonder when the day ends.

"Hello, everyone. This is Tricky Bird. I have been appointed to coordinate the Reflections period this evening. For the benefit of any visitors among us, this period is devoted to sharing any discoveries, difficulties, or insights we may have attained during the day. All are free to participate. The channel is open."

"I would like to say one thing. I have been very upset. This thing with my parents' divorce has hurt me. I stopped caring about a lot of things. I just wanted to crawl into a corner, or if I came out I wanted to hurt someone. Anyway I have been trying to find a way out. I have tried working on it directly in psychodrama. I have drawn pictures. I have danced it. I have tried many things and many of you have helped me for which I am grateful. But there was still something wrong. Today I think I identified it. It was my attitude. I was assuming that my reaction was something evil and sick and had to be wiped out. Everything I tried was like a stain remover, but the stain remained. It got paler but it was still there."

"That was all wrong. I was in sensory awakening class this morning going through a set of routines and suddenly when I wasn't even thinking about it, an inner voice said, "If you wiped it out before you learned from it, the whole experience would be wasted." There was nothing emotional about it. Just like a voice on a tape giving a lecture. But I suddenly got a cold chill and just lay there feeling paralyzed. I have spent the day concentrating on my reactions to the situation. I am not trying to weaken them, just to drink them to the full. And the surprising thing [he begins to cry], the surprising thing is that I feel much better."

"I have been studying the control of attention. In particular I have been pursuing the exercises involving the reconstruction of the past, each night recalling the day in reverse. I have been at it for three months. Last night I decided to introduce a new variation. I decided to recall the next day backward as though it had already happened. Before I began, I used a little self-hypnosis to convince myself that what I visualized had actually happened and was not a dream. Then I spoke out loud what I saw so that it could be recorded. Three of the events that I remembered happened today. I don't know what it means. Did I make them happen? Did I simply sense that they must happen from an understanding of the situation, or was it precognition? Frankly, I don't care. I am not going to talk any more about it until I have worked on it for a few weeks, but if anyone else would care to try, I would certainly be interested in the results."

"This is Flabby Herodotus. I have been continuing my studies on how school children used to waste most of their time. I have had an insight. They were never really supposed to do much. A similar assumption exists in this school but in the opposite direction. We assume, without recognizing it, that we are in a situation of negative infinity, not a closed circle but a saddle whose edges recede forever into space without ever turning on themselves. Knowing that there is no end, all our efforts seem small and we are continually caught up in extending them. I have not yet identified how this assumption was generated, but I shall continue my investigations through sampling of FNC information layers and selective interviews with teachers."

"I have been studying the process of answering multiple choice questions without knowing anything about the subject matter. Up until now I have simply been exploring distributions of correct responses and the elimination of obviously unlikely answers. As you know, response categories are not selected at random unless a randomizer is employed in the placement of the correct response, which is generally the case today. Further, no test maker, no matter how painstaking, can make all responses equally likely, an assumption upon which the test model is based. Therefore, it is possible by the inspection of the alternatives and the employment of a specialized probability table to raise score levels to a degree significant at the .01 level (that is, they would not be likely to occur by chance more than one in one hundred times). A few days ago I hit on the idea of using ESP techniques. Today I employed Astral Head for purposes of predicting right answers after having employed the other approaches. The results were excellent. Of course, AH is an excellent subject, but I thought you all might be interested. . . ."

"I have been interested in . . ."

"I was going to say . . ."

"You first."

"All right. I have been working with the parent relations group. You remember the last report. We were analyzing the kinds of subjects that really send parents off their rocker. We have done a content analysis of these subjects and come up with several principles which might interest you since they probably refer to contact with outside persons in general. First is the double standard. There is a lot that parents believe in for kids in general, that they won't accept for their child in particular. Specifically, sex education is accepted as a matter of course (by the vast majority of our parents) but a good deal of concern is expressed about the possibility of premature experimentation. They find our operation in full view of everyone somewhat reassuring. But the behavior of some of the teachers has shaken them up. They have conceived of the idea of some general conspiracy, mass orgies among the small fry. Another principle working in the opposite direction is that if he is mine, he can't be wrong. They lack objectivity in evaluating data on their child. This is not unexpected but has led to a suggestion of a course for parents on "learning to see your child again. A third principle which is more insidious is 'I want the best for my child but I am threatened by his achievements.' This leads to subtle forms of undermining the child's self-confidence and emotional health, or polarizing him into a too uncritical defense of the school. All of which is to say that one part of a family system cannot be altered without affecting the other. The parts that are untouched must exert an inhibiting influence on the changing elements if the equilibrium is to remain relatively stable."

"I was going to say before that I have been studying teaching programs in terms of Laban's ideas of physical movement. I have been attempting to translate his scheme of basic physical actions into different types of steps in programming, trying to create 'slashing' items, 'floating' items, 'dabbing' items. I seem to be having some success. I don't know where it is all leading. Perhaps the items should be viewed as part of an evolving or recurrent pattern. Imagine a composition of program steps that has aesthetic beauty as well as informational content. . . ."

"I have adopted an idea from an approach used by a sect active in the 1950s. They used to leave notes to remind themselves of certain simple actions they had intended to take. I haven't done that. What I do is summarize my progress in a number of key areas—English, mathematics, movement and particularly spelling. I put it right in front of me so it's the first thing I see when I wake up. It helps me to get right into things. It sounds pretty stupid, but it seems to work."

"This is Crooked Egg Head. I have put together two ideas. I was reading about mass learning and about marathon group experiences. I decided to pick a subject and do nothing but study it for twenty-four hours straight. I picked something new for me, Spanish. I may have heard it spoken, but I didn't know a word. After twenty-four hours the tests show that I got through the first year and a half. But I don't think I would want to go through that again in a hurry. I used a variety of things to keep me going strong and awake, but right now everything is getting fuzzy. Maybe it was stupid. Let's see what I remember when I wake up."

"I need one good empathizer with E rating 93 or better. I am studying rat maze behavior, duplicating some of the classic experiments. It seems to me that some of the results are ambiguous. If we only had some idea of what the rats were thinking and feeling, their behavior might become more understandable. So if there is a good empathizer in the house who wants to take on a new species, I need you."

"I think that concluded the Reflections period today. Regular evening activities will begin in ten minutes. This is Tricky Bird signing off."

Now what? Nobody ever seems to eat around here. I'm starved.

"Hey. When do you eat here?"
"You hungry?"
"Don't you have supper?"
"We eat all the time in the garden. Just take what you want and eat."

Why didn't anyone tell me? But then nobody tells me anything. In the garden I hear some voices. I see some kids eating, but where is the food?

"How do you like our eating garden?"
"It's very nice, but where is the food?"
"This is a project of design and ecology classes with a little help from engineering. AEG (automated eating garden) complete with tropical plants, Japanese-type rocks, and hidden waterfalls. You can even get a sunburn. But take off your shoes if you go on the grass, and be careful of the flowers. They take a lot of work."
"But the food? Where is it?"
"You have to push buttons. Everything is frozen. Kitchen detail makes the food. Then it goes on a conveyer belt into the freezer section. You push the button, it goes into the radar oven for a few minutes and comes up ready. We get to vote on menus once a month. Push that button over there under the rock. I helped scrape the carrots. If you taste any blood, it's mine. Enjoy your food. I am going to eat dessert under the waterfall and listen to the sirens."

"What is that?"

"I don't know just what it is, but it sure does something to you. Just reach under the rock and get your food when you want it. Throw everything in the garbage inside that hollow tree trunk when you finish."

The kids cook all their own food. I hope it's edible. Probably franks and potato chips with ice cream for dessert. No, three vegetables, homemade soup, salad, and some kind of beef. It looks good. Is that corn bread? No. It tastes of coconut. I guess if you have to live with what you cook, it comes out all right. Must produce some strange ideas of role confusion. Would a woman ever be willing to be the cook if she went to this school? But I don't even know who does the cooking. Maybe only girls do it. Maybe only people who want to do it. That's probably what happens. You have to help some way, but you get to choose what you want or what you think would be good for you. I'm sure they have it all worked out. I suppose I could have come here anytime to get something to eat, if I had only known about it. If you could eat anytime, you wouldn't need much space.

Doesn't the school ever close? What could go on this evening? The parents must be disturbed. Maybe they are delighted to have their kids so occupied. They aren't trying to get rid of them. The kids must want to stay or they would go home.

Now what's going on? They are moving all the walls out of the way. There must be about 200 kids here. Who is that getting up? She looks very clean and impressive. She moves like a dancer, maybe the movement teacher.

"All the sounds have been turned off. For the next fifteen minutes there will be silence. During that time anyone who feels so inclined will have the chance to dance his day, to move in whatever way he wants, to transmit to others some quality, some experience which was meaningful for him. If you have nothing to say, say nothing, but don't hold back. One of you, a few, many, all. It doesn't matter. I have some simple instruments here. If you need them, take them. In fifteen minutes I will ring a loud gong and you will know that it is over. Thank you. Begin when you are ready."

No one moves. I hope to God I am not supposed to join in. There goes a small boy making for a tom-tom. What a strange beat. It has a yearning quality.

A young girl with long red hair starts to move. Just running through the building, her hair streaming behind her like a flame. She rears back and collapses on the floor.

Two young boys get up. They seem to be playing some game, combining hide and seek with cops and robbers. They are using people as objects, leaning on them, putting one foot or an arm on them, falling over them. They grab another boy and pull him along the floor by his hands. He hangs there like a wet rag.

The red-haired girl gets up and finds an instrument that gives out high glassy notes when she hits it. She and the boy with the tom-tom seem to ignore each other. They both are starting to move, each to their own notes and rhythm, in different parts of the building.

The children begin to get up to move with them, some eagerly, some as if it is against their will. They are drawn into it, graceful, stumbling, separately, and in small groups. The little boy with his tom-tom looks very serious and quite old. The girl seems oblivious of her following. She strikes the notes harder and higher.

I don't know what all this is supposed to symbolize. It doesn't seem to have any particular content. An older boy gets up, walks to the center of the room and begins to whirl around. He seems very deliberate, holding his arms in a definite fashion, one up and the other to his side. He looks like a whirling dervish. He gets faster and faster but never out of control. A few other children begin to move around him, running, turning, twisting. Does he even see them? He seems to have stabilized his motion. He may even be slowing down.

What a strange and immense scene. The whole building looks so large with the walls folded away. Above, the spheres glow, shifting their colors like an extraterrestrial life form, observing the human children dance and noting the strange patterns that they create as they go along.

No one is bothering me. I am grateful for that. But I almost feel like joining in. I am a stranger. I would be very awkward. It would be ridiculous. But it wouldn't hurt to stand up and maybe move around a bit. I seem to want to stretch up very high . . . higher . . . and just spin once or twice. I have all this energy. I want to race around like a berserk machine making a mechanical motion. It does it all by itself. The motion goes on without me. I seem to be full of anger and tension. I would love to beat on something or stamp on the floor. I must look like a madman, but who is there to notice? This thing really wants to come out of me. Does it have anything to do with me or not? I don't know. I don't care.

Everyone seems to be joining together now, forming some large irregular figure. Starting far, far apart, on the outskirts of the building, and now 200 people are coming together with growing speed, faster and faster and meeting together in a fantastic heap . . . people laughing, sighing, breathing, someone crying.

Was that the gong? Yes. It sounds again.

"For the next minute would you all make some kind of sound to express how you feel. It does not have to be loud or soft. Don't pay attention to others. Make your own sound. Begin!"

In the next instant an indescribable sound sweeps through the total building. It is like a great organ giving forth a vast array of tones, the combined effect of which no builder could ever anticipate. The variety is astonishing. I stopped breathing. Just to listen. Forgetting everything. After perhaps forty-five seconds I breathe in with a deep wheezing noise. That is my own sound.

A high gong sounds through everything. And quiet is restored.

A man gets up, pauses, looks around in every direction.

"Now that the evening has come it is time to resolve situations that we have not handled or fulfilled during the day. We do not want to be haunted by them in our sleep. Look around you. Seek out people with whom you have unfinished business. Whatever it is, pleasant or unpleasant, complete it. When you do, move on. Don't be haunted later on by what you fail to do now. Begin."

I move toward the eating garden. I doubt that anyone has business with me. I just want to watch, but what am I watching? I see a young boy and girl running together from perhaps fifty feet across the room, hugging each other . . . a girl slaps someone in the face . . . it looks like a teacher. Someone screams in someone else's ear "You stupid bitch." It is strange, wild. People seem to know what they are doing, but I cannot tell why they are doing it. I watch. Will they feel better? Does it help tomorrow to let it out today? Do I have anything I would want to do? I suppose I would like Einstein Monster to come out of the arena. I would like to see some of the people again to ask more questions or tell them that I understand more clearly.

As I look around, I realize that my first impression was wrong. Many people are sitting together in pairs and small groups deep in conversation. I walk around the room listening to snatches of conversation.

". . . so angry when you didn't even listen to what. . . ."

"Stupid, that's what gets me. If it were for some purpose, but you just. . . ."

"I don't mind, honestly, but most people would just think that all you were interested in was. . . ."

". . . don't care what you say. It shows all over you. Stop smiling, it. . . ."

"No, no, no. Is that good enough? Can't you believe that I really. . . ."

". . . dear. It doesn't matter to me what you do. Only leave me out of it. . . ."

". . . be easier. Everyone wants you to feel at ease. We don't mean. . . ."

On and on, everyone so intent and oblivious of everyone else. Some wandering around like me, lost spirits, unsure of what they want, afraid of doing it, or not finding who they are looking for. It is a scene out of purgatory. Could they do this every night? It doesn't seem possible. That looks like the meditation teacher. He is coming toward me. I am in for it.

"There you are. Don't look so concerned. I don't have much on my mind, only I said a lot to you. It bothered me. Maybe you didn't mind, but I did. Afterward, I regretted it. I couldn't help myself."

"You don't have to apologize."

"But I know that I could have done the same thing with half the energy. I get overheated when someone from the outside comes in. They seem so dense to me, and I get so eager to get through to them. I wish I could be cooler."

"Don't trouble yourself. It was all right."

"You say that. But I know better. I am supposed to be teaching awareness and control to these kids. I have to have it myself. I don't mind that a few of the kids can do things I'll never be able to do, but if I don't set some kind of example, where am I? Excuse me now. I see someone over there."

He goes, looking calmer and stronger. He didn't do much for me, but he feels better. I am glad. Naturally he feels better than I do. I didn't resolve anything. He did.

"Hello, Little Father."

"Do I know you?"

"No, but I have been feeling a little guilty because we left you so much on your own. I am Wise Owl. I could probably answer some of your questions, if you still have them."

"I wish you had come sooner."

"We wanted you to form your own impressions. I am here now. Don't waste time on the past. You will be leaving soon."

"Will I?"

"Yes. I think so."

"All right. How can you possibly function without a schedule?"

"There is a schedule, but you may not have sensed it. The younger children during their first two years are led through an intensive human potentialities curriculum. Their classes meet at definite times each day. This occupies perhaps two-thirds of their time. During the rest they do homework and become acquainted with the arena. After the first two years, the program is much more flexible. Students can attend any class they wish or none at all. The basic work in any class is elementary, but advanced students can add to the class and benefit from it. Sometimes they take over the instruction. Some classes such as the one on integrating human functions continue through the third year. But we have found that after the first two years, we tend to become a group of equals pooling our resources to ends of mutual interest. Status is not a big thing here. A person is judged on the basis of what he can do, which changes from situation to situation."

"I suppose the important thing is the result. What happens to your students?"

"They have a very good record, but we are not fully responsible for that. The kind of parents that would want their children to be in a school like this must be unusual. It is too soon for us to evaluate the long-range effects, but the immediate impact is remarkable. Many of our advanced students are doing second-year college work in their areas of interest. Their intellectual attainment is generally very high. People never realized the incredible inefficiency of the traditional school. It was like trying to get cars with weak batteries started on a cold morning. Kids naturally want to learn. You have to work at it to turn them into suspicious resistant cripples who resist learning.

"But we are not overjoyed with our level of intellectual success. We are relieved that we attain it, but if that were all that had happened, we would have failed. Our aim is to create whole growing organisms. This is a new undertaking. A lot of people have thought about it, written about it, talked to others about it. We are doing it, day by day, using every approach that seems effective. I don't myself have much faith in any particular thing. There are so many factors all continuously varying at different rates. It is the accumulation of influences all directed toward a general end that slowly creates the power to which we all relate and from which we draw in varying degrees."

"The school is alive. It is an organism. Its brain may be the basement, but it stretches everywhere through the lives of the people who enter it, work in it, and grow from it. I hope I don't sound as though I am trying to sell it to you. That is the temptation. I don't want to do that. Because it is so easy to create the illusion of something great. The reality is different. It is painful, draining, sometimes wild, often beautiful, but this is no place for a lazy person. Every difficulty is exposed. Weaknesses are rooted out. Very little escapes the accumulated knowledge and understanding of others and of FNC."

"Do you have any private life or does this absorb your whole identity?"

"What is a private life? Is it a set of relationships that are intimate but not task-oriented. I think the whole idea of private and public is misleading. When men divide up their activities in segregated situations, then you need a private life to balance the public one; but when virtually all aspects of existence are open to understanding and growth, the distinction breaks down.

"Do I have intimate relations with others here? Of course. How could it be otherwise. We love each other, hate, are indifferent to, sometimes all toward the same person. It keeps evolving, deepening, maturing."

"This is such a closed environment. Don't you generate all kinds of emotional difficulties? What about premature sex?"

"What about premature calculus? Every function has its own natural period of development, but they are not independent of each other. If the person is healthy, there is a natural integration. Sex is usually a problem because it is divorced from other aspects of human behavior. Is sunshine a problem? Only if you stay out in it too long without protection.

"Our kids are precocious. They are precocious about everything. They are curious, scientific, emotional. The problems they have about sex are mostly those that adults put on them. Remember that we train them not only in expression but also control. It extends not only to the mind, emotions, and sensations, but to sex. Long ago men discovered that sensation and sex, like fine wine, take time and atmosphere to be properly savored. A person who swallows wine like water is uncultivated. These children learn to respect sex as a power of life. They learn to be wary of its deviousness and their own vulnerability. Have you seen any sexual problems? Are our older students screwing in the halls? There is no privacy. We don't grow promiscuous people here. The more in touch a person is with his own nature, the more selective he becomes. It is the driven person who goes from relationship to relationship, never really satisfied by any of them."

"Isn't there anything wrong with what you are doing?"

"A great deal. All that I hope, all that any of us hopes, is that each passing day reveals to the light some undiscovered problem, some unsuspected source of decay, some insight into a new possibility. When that happens, we know we are headed in the right direction. Each day, if we approach it right, is a complete event. And in the evening we die."

"That sounds somewhat dramatic."

"In our culture no one knows how to die. We ignore the subject as long as possible and then turn it over to the professionals. But you can't hire someone to die for you. So we study how to die along with everything else."

"Don't the parents get nervous?"

"We don't use the word 'die.' We talk of "letting go," "surrender," "living in the present," "not being deterred by the mistakes of the past," but truthfully we teach people how to die.

"Nothing grows without something else dying. Nature shows us this in a thousand ways. It is not bad or threatening or dangerous. The worst and stupidest death is that of an unprepared human being coming to the end of his days. Death ought to be an inner event, not an inevitable outcome of physiological exhaustion. We do not know how to depart. When you leave here, can you really let it go and move on to the next thing open and empty, or will you trail us behind you in a series of unresolved feelings and observations?

"Each day when the sun goes down, the world goes to sleep. That, too, is death. The morning is birth. The idea is old. We built upon its reality. Most people in psychotherapy don't know how to let the past die. It haunts them until it distorts the present. They learn slowly, painfully, and expensively. In this place we put our ghosts to rest as fast as we can."

"I think I understand, but one thing worries me. This place seems to me so special that it could never be duplicated. It wouldn't be economically feasible. The conditions wouldn't be parallel. If that's so, what general purpose does it serve except for the students who are lucky enough to be here?"

"I agree. It would be of little use except for that. But I don't agree that it cannot be transferred. You are blinded by the technology. The arena is a sophisticated toy. It cost a lot as an initial investment but the more it is used, the more the cost decreases. We have it because we could get the money for it. People will pay for machines. But we don't need it."

"You don't need it!"

"Not really. Most of the things that really impress you are frills. We don't need the special effects, the domes, the audio-visual apparatus. All we really need is simple flexible space. And that is the cheapest thing there is. But cost is very deceptive. People will invest endlessly in machines for destruction and the prevention of destruction. Economy is a state of mind.

"Do you have any notion how much money we save by doing everything ourselves? This is probably the most economic educational operation you have ever seen. It doesn't matter. No one demands it of us. It is the outcome of our own approach. We are proud of our relative self-sufficiency. Even the building was planned by the students."

"I didn't know that."

"Not these students, an earlier generation. At first we just had little temporary shelters, a kind of heated geodesic dome made up of materials that could be thrown away or used later. We lived in those for two years. During that time we started the internal curriculum and designed the building. We used consultants in design and engineering, but we did the work ourselves. They answered our questions, but we made the decisions. The hardest part was getting the parents and school board to agree to let us live like that for two years. The kids loved it. Those were the pioneer days.

"Just about everything you see was the outcome of what went on those first two years. Imagine a building designed by students, a place to house their work, an environment for their own development. It is a really beautiful idea. We even did some of the construction. We couldn't do it all. We had some trouble with unions, but we worked it out."

"How?"

"Actually, we had taken the precaution to admit the children of several union officials to the school. They couldn't resist their own kids. You may wonder how the students had time to learn anything with all this going on, but they did. Everything was used for something else. Mixing concrete was used in chemistry and movement class as well as perception and sensory awareness. Negotiating with workmen was carried over into social competence class and empathy work. Sometimes I feel limited by what we have created, but it couldn't have been made more flexible, and we don't have to stay here. Is there anything else?"

"There are lots of things, a whole history of events, but you look like you have to go somewhere."

"I have something to do, but that concerns you, so it can wait for one more question, if you have one."

"What happens in the evening? When does the place ever go to sleep?"

"You have seen some of the things we do. We reserve the evening for activities involving everyone. After that there is a variety of special activities—planning groups, governing groups. Then people go their own way. Some stay to study for a few hours. Most drift home. A few stay here and work all night. Einstein Monster watches over the machine. The arena is never out of use. A certain proportion of the students prefer to work at night. The atmosphere is different."

"I like to work at night myself. What happens now?"

"We have prepared a show for your benefit. This is a product of the creativity and social competence classes. You didn't know you have been a project?"

"Only this morning. What do I do?"

"Just sit down over here and watch the wall. When it is all over, you can leave. I don't think you will want to stay. Goodby. It has been good to talk with you."

"Thank you. Goodby."

The wall is turning into a screen. There I am, coming in the door. That must be this morning. And I thought I was alone. Do I always look so stupid when I am thoughtful? My posture is horrible. I look paranoid. I guess that was how I felt.

I must be smelling the shoe leather and pickled beets. My God, I can smell them now. That must be part of it. This all seems so very long ago. I remember thinking the sound shells looked like great rock forms hollowed out by the glaciers, or something on the moon. I was so struck with the newness of it all, bemused, trying to read the minds of the people who created it and lived there, while they had me under observation.

Now the camera work is getting interesting . . . close-ups of my hands . . . split screen effects put me in two places at once. What are those voices?

"He is thinking about the domes and wondering how they are heated."

"He is wondering where everyone is."

"He is looking for the classrooms. He thinks it all looks like an elephant's graveyard. He thinks that" (the voices fade).

That must be the empathy class watching me and commenting.

There I sit with my eyes closed. And now she notices me, hesitates, and comes over. That was such an unexpected and nice thing to do. She looks so competent. Not a very pretty girl but very warm. Animals would feel secure in her presence. I can still feel her touch. And I never saw her again, the whole rest of the day. I might not even have remembered her, and that was the nicest thing that happened all day. Look at that big smile on my face.

"I feel very helpless with my eyes closed. I am at your mercy."
"Do you object to that?"
"Not really. I am enjoying it."

Listen to my neck crack. Wow . . . Another moment, and there she goes.

That must be the parent. What have they done to the sound track? They must have doubled its speed. We sound like two pigeons. Now the young janitor.

"Are you a high school drop-out?"
"No. I am a student. It is our building. We take care of it."

I don't suppose I really believed him. If he mopped the floor, he had to be a janitor or a student janitor earning extra money. Why was I so irritated just because he didn't conform to my expectation?

It goes on and on.

"May I go to class with you?"
"Yes. I was supposed to find a subject."
"You mean me."
"I'm afraid so. Maybe the ESP class is trying to read your mind. Maybe the ethics class is diagnosing your value system. Maybe the role class is improvising a scene between you and your wife. Are you married?"
"What do they call you?"
"Little Bean. I think we will call you Dumb Head. Goodby, Dumb Head. Don't look so angry. You don't even know what it means."
"Well, tell me then." Tell me then . . . tell me then (it reverberates until it loses meaning.)
"This is an improvisation, actually."

"I can try, but aren't you all a little old for this. It sounds more like six year olds."

"We are six year olds."

"I'm seven."

"And I am one hundred and seventeen. My name is Toddles."

"We hurt his feelings. He is angry."

"I wouldn't be in the same room with him."

"But old Mr. Dumb Head. He was only ventilating his feelings."

"Hello. I am Mr. . . . I mean Dumb Head. How are you feeling?"

"Much better, DH. I was just recalling. . . ."

". . . It is an organism and we are its parts."

"We use names to help them remember who they are. Our names change when the people change."

"Then imagine yourself shouting as loud as you can, "Why do they call me Dumb Head? and after you do that. . . ."

"All right. You may be stronger than I am, but you are a bully."

"You do what I tell you to do. I don't care what you think as long as you do it."

"YOU ARE A DUMB HEAD."

"My name is Dumb Head."

"My name is Little Thunder . . . I think you should be called Little Father . . . Go down to the end of the hall and push the wall. . . ."

"I don't want to leave. That's why they call me Monster. I am ten years old, but I have a high intelligence quotient. This is my cocoon."

". . . This is a class in introductory meditation. We were doing Zazen. . . . You lack a center in yourself."

"I don't know about that."

"Don't be insulted. Very few people do."

"This school was created as a place for growth. . . . The mind needs ideas, the heart emotional flow, the body action, the soul cosmic contact. . . . I didn't mean to talk so long."

"The day is a necklace of delights.
Each gem an event hidden in the heart of fire. . . ."

"Suddenly I got a cold chill and just lay there feeling paralyzed."

"This is Flabby Herodotus. I am continuing my studies on how school children used to spend their day doing so little. I have had an insight. . . ."

"We were analyzing the kinds of subjects that really send parents off their rocker. We have done a content analysis. . . ."

"This is Crooked Egg Head. I have put together two ideas."

"This is Dribbly Nose Edison. I want a group of five volunteers."

"I need one good empathizer with E rating of 93 or better. I am studying. . . ."

"When do you eat here?"

"Why? Are you hungry?"

"For the next fifteen minutes there will be silence. During that time anyone who feels so inclined will have the chance to dance his day."

"For the next minute would you all make some kind of sound to express how you feel."

"What happens to your students? . . . Do you have any private life? . . . What about premature sex? . . . Is there anything wrong with what you are doing? . . . Don't the parents get nervous? . . . What happens in the evening? . . ."

"Just sit down over here and watch the wall. . . . Goodby."

She was right. I cannot stay. I must go as I came, walking down the hall, through the entrance, and finally into the night air and the still sleeping world.

EPILOGUE

NUMBER TWO: I have heard enough of this.

NUMBER ONE: Who are you?

NUMBER TWO: You asked for me to come in person, so here I am.

NUMBER THREE: Let's get started.

NUMBER TWO: Let's stop!

NUMBER ONE: It can't be stopped.

NUMBER THREE: I want to know what to do next.

NUMBER ONE: Begin to work and have a little faith.

NUMBER TWO: You don't think you are going to get away with this.

NUMBER ONE: How will you stop us?

NUMBER TWO: There are any number of ways. You will need funds. You will need official support. They will not be forthcoming. Rumors can be spread. You are incredibly naive.

NUMBER THREE: Why do you want to poison the fountain?

NUMBER TWO: Human beings were not meant to be free. It is all right for a few dreamers, but do you seriously think that we can permit youth to find their own way into the future. Our whole complex edifice, the hidden sources of our power, would be subtly undermined.

NUMBER THREE: What can I do to help?

NUMBER ONE: I already told you. Begin to use what is already there. Grow stronger. Follow the path as it unfolds before you.

NUMBER THREE: I am afraid that it is too late to begin.

196

NUMBER ONE: You may be right. Every turn of history suggests that our sinister friend with embittered eyes will win. I am not naive.

NUMBER THREE: But if you believe that, what is the use?

NUMBER ONE: I believe that it will not be easy, but I also know that the possibilities are staggering. If you want to spend the rest of your life in a decaying routine, let us part here. Join me if you can. But don't hold me back.

NUMBER TWO: I am going to enjoy watching you being crushed to dust.

NUMBER ONE: I have already beaten you.

NUMBER TWO: The battle has not started.

NUMBER ONE: You work most effectively in secret. But we are not alone.

NUMBER TWO: Of course we are alone. I had this room thoroughly investigated before I came here.

NUMBER ONE: You are wrong. We are not alone. The ancient barriers are breaking. You can hear the approach of rushing waters sweeping away rotting walls.

NUMBER TWO: You are a dreamer.

NUMBER ONE: Listen! You can hear the water. With a new age comes an ancient opportunity. Man will be fulfilled.

NUMBER TWO: You are a religious fanatic!

NUMBER THREE: What does this have to do with education?

NUMBER ONE: We are observed. Don't you sense it? That is what makes the vital difference.

NUMBER TWO: I have taken elaborate precautions against such a possibility.

NUMBER THREE: I can sense something. People, listening, watching. Perhaps we are not alone. . . .

APPENDIXES: *The Research Study on Strategies for Cultivating Human Potential*[1]

STUDYING BEHAVIORAL STRATEGIES

Studying behavioral strategies may be thought of as exploring a new continent. We know it exists but are ignorant of its boundaries and geographic features. In the present instance a body of relevant data was available, which consisted of a description and analysis of over fifty methods for cultivating personal growth. A list of these approaches is given in Appendix Two. These methods formed a useful point of departure because of their diversity of ends and variety of means. Representing a sample from the larger population of behavior change methods, they were examined in order to prepare a representative list of behavioral strategies. This was not always easy because the originators of these techniques were often more interested in speculation and lengthy case histories than in the simple description of what the practitioners do. Nevertheless, an inspection of these methods did provide a variety of component strategies helpful in the present investigation.

In addition to this basic source of information a number of eclectic descriptions of behavioral strategies were reviewed.[1] These included:

> *Joy,* by William C. Schutz (Grove, 1967); *You Are Not the Target,* by Laura A. Huxley (Farrar, Straus and Giroux, 1963); *Human Potentialities: The Challenge and the Promise,* edited by Herbert A. Otto (Green, 1968); *Ways of Growth,* edited by Herbert A. Otto and John Mann (Grossman, 1968); *Venture with Ideas,* by Kenneth Walker (Pellegrini & Cudahy, 1952); *The Stanislavski System,* by Sonia Moore (Macmillan, 1965); *Persuasion,* by H. I. Abelson (Springer, 1959); *Changing Human Behavior,* by John Mann (Scribner's, 1965).

From these sources, about 200 strategies were identified. They are listed in Appendix Three in the order in which they were identified. There are so many strategies in this list that it is difficult to assess or appreciate what they represent. For this reason it may be helpful to examine a few of them in detail before trying to characterize the total collection in a more general sense.

Analysis of Selected Strategies

For purposes of this analysis the first twenty strategies listed in Appendix Three were chosen for further study. No attempt was made to obtain a random sample. The original listing of strategies was not guided by any particular criteria, so that those selected vary widely in focus and depth and we considered them characteristic of the total group. Our purpose was simply to explore the kinds of thoughts, hunches, and speculations that a more detailed examination of specific actions incorporated in these strategies might suggest.

Strategy One—*Secrecy*

Secrecy exists on various conceptual levels—from the sociological analysis of secret societies to the psychological study of individual forgetfulness, i.e., keeping a secret from oneself. Secrecy involves an element of discipline, i.e., controlling what one says. It logically precedes the strategy of passing on what one has learned. One effect of secrecy is to keep energy within a given social system so that it can accumulate and resonate rather than seep away. An analogy can be made with a growing plant. Energy must be accumulated until the plant grows and the fruit ripens. It can then be picked without injury to the plant.

Strategies Two and Three—
Time Orientation and the Use of Time Limits

There are many ways in which time can be controlled or altered. One can focus on a particular phase of time. The past is emphasized in psychoanalysis, the present in Gestalt therapy, and the future in goal setting and other problem-solving procedures. It is interesting to characterize different combinations of time orientations. Past-present represents the goalless individual with a memory. Past-future has the timeless quality of historical inevitability—what has been will be. Present-future is oriented toward attainable goals and has a positive problem-solving orientation.

The duration of time can be divided in a number of ways—length of a session, number of sessions or duration of a total experience, timing of interventions of a particular kind, utilization of certain times of the day for particular activities, making schedules, and planning in general.

Any plan must be projected in future time and act as a frame of reference for present action. In contrast, "undoing Karma" in Laura Huxley's sense is action on the past.[2] Most psychotherapy incorporates this kind of action.

Time is related to motion, i.e., motion is the expression of action in the unfolding present. It is the dynamic translation of time into sensation. Without such inner and outer motion, time would be meaningless. One of the objectives of work on oneself is to enter time, to become centered in the eternal now of the expanded present so that time unfolds around one in every direction.

Strategy Four—*Establishing Connections*

Connections can be established between different points on the time scale (e.g., present and future through planning), or through different levels of experience existing at the same time (e.g., sense of inner tension and awareness of outer action). Connecting is a folding action that bridges walls and barriers, brings together that which we thought should be separated, and causes us to redefine our boundaries. When the connection is made, a flow of energy occurs that may transform the relation between the points that are connected. Such an experience can act as a shock, particularly if fear was the motivating force for avoiding such a relation in the past.

The connection itself usually occurs through a heightened awareness, as exemplified by the strategy of the Gestalt therapist who draws attention to disconnected fragments of behavior. By bringing them into awareness, he helps to re-establish the connection between them.

Strategy Five—*Concretizing*

Concretizing involves moving from the vague to the specific, from the abstract principle to the direct sensation. Concretizing is closely allied to creativity. To build a new product all the details must be specified. Stanislavski spoke of the importance of physicalization in helping the actor to build a new part.[3] The process of learning is closely related to making vague ideas concrete. Making practical applications of general discoveries also uses this general strategy.

Concretizing is a direct process. Haiku poetry and Zen painting are examples of simple concrete imagery used to express subtle psychological states. Concretizing is a redefinition of a situation in a direction in terms of which correct and incorrect responses can be given. The notion of strategies is itself a concretization of subtle behavior change procedures.

Strategy Six—*Splitting Attention*

Attention can be divided between different tasks of the same kind (typing and observing the paper in the typewriter), different kinds (typing and listening to music), different levels (typing and observing muscular reactions), and different determinants of experience (sensing time and feeling space).

What is the effect of conscious splitting of attention? In general the man whose attention is successfully split cannot be easily influenced because he is occupied elsewhere. In addition, splitting enables ideas and actions to emerge without undue personal editing for the same reason. Thus, it is an active alternative to simply letting go.[4] In Spolin's theater games the use of divided attention is a central principle.[5] One never does an outer exercise without an inner point of concentration.

Strategy Seven—*Forcing*

Forcing is the opposite of letting go. Any technique forces that places the subject in an uncomfortable dilemma. It is one end of a dimension that varies from allowing, observing, suggesting, showing, urging to actively forcing. Demmerlie forces muscular realignment in his structural reintegration process.[6] Schutz forces interpersonal confrontation in his approach to encounter group functioning.[7] The same strategy is used in a number of the more dramatic behavior change approaches, from the Zen Master hitting the incorrect student with his staff to the physiological and psychological stress of "brain washing."

It is necessary to distinguish learning theory studies of the coercive use of pain and punishment from forcing, which utilizes pain, paradox, and uncertainty within a single context such as Zen. The administration of pain for failure to resolve a paradox is different from using it as a punishment for a moral wrong or for incorrect behavior.

Strategy Eight—*Spreading*

The Golden Flower exercise is a good example of the spreading of sensation through guided awareness.[8] Does this approach work on other levels? Does the process of becoming aware of thought help to change or clarify it? Does the use of free association involve the extension of emotional awareness? If so, awareness is, in this case, the tool rather than the objective.

Spreading is a gentle process. One allows awareness to dwell for a brief period and then removes it, like a light on a photographic plate or a catalyst that has done its work. Moderation is required. Too little attention does not produce an effect. Too much may undo it.

Strategy Nine—*Flowing*

Flowing is closely related to spreading. Flow of human action cannot occur without awareness. To have flowing movements the individual must sense how his muscles feel, what they want to express, where they want to go. This experience has nothing to do with intelligence or emotion. But ideas, emotions, and sensations as well as movement can flow. Sex can flow.

Once such a process has begun, resistances to flow are immediately obvious. One of the underlying questions in the use of component strategies is how to reestablish such a flow when it is blocked.

Strategy Ten—*Least Possible Effort*

Making the least possible effort is one of the basic principles of the Chinese system of exercises called Tai Chi Chuan. Performing actions in this way requires that one be aware of his actions because tension usually is unconscious. It takes awareness to release tension, and the act of release improves awareness. A new kind of flowing movement occurs when this releasing action has passed a certain point and an enhancement of physical sensations also occurs.

Strategy Eleven—*Nonresistance*

This strategy is also clearly illustrated in Tai Chi Chuan in the exercise in which one man pushes another. If the second man remains completely relaxed and internally quiet, no force that is exerted on him can throw him off balance. This exercise is the outer expression of "turning the other cheek." Of course, nonresistance can be emotional and intellectual as well as physical, but the physical action is a particularly expressive indicator of the inner state.

Strategy Twelve—*Intervening*

Intervention requires that one interfere with a continuing process. It differs from interaction in that it comes from outside the immediate situation and often carries an added weight of authority derived from the larger social system of which the immediate action is a part. An intervention is a shock that is accepted because of its authority and surprise. The person who intervenes supplies crucial action. Even if his words appear casual, the effect is not.

What is involved in making an intervention? First, we must be willing to take the responsibility for the effect of our actions. Second, it requires a definite effort. Third, timing is particularly important. Finally, we must be convinced that one is right and that the action is necessary.

Strategies Thirteen, Fourteen, and Fifteen—*Touching*

Is touching strictly physical? Symbolically it expresses affection, support, intimacy, nonverbal communication, and healing. The language of the body attributes different meanings to touching different parts of the body. Sex is an important determinant of this language, but other things are involved such as role, care given to different parts of the body, custom, and the like.

Can emotions, sensations, or thoughts be touched in any sense? In order to touch an inner experience we must be detached from it. We can touch our dreams only when we are awake.

Strategy Sixteen—*Alteration of Imagery*

Imagining is a mental activity. It may be approached in a variety of different ways and is most systematically developed in the psychosynthesis system of Assagioli.[9] It can vary from the visualization of an object's shape or color to the creation of a full fantasy world. Any action can occur through imagining without a parallel action in the real social world. Two people can imagine a fight without fighting (and experience many of the same effects) or imagine love without loving.

In one sense imagining is a purely projective device. As in a dream, everything that occurs is derived from the individual. In another sense imagining is creative and to some extent self-rewarding as it takes hold.

The relation between imagining and acting needs to be explored. For example, can we accomplish a difficult task if we imagine ourself successfully accomplishing it? Can we visualize a continuing emotion and understand it better in the process? Can we visualize a part of one's body and does this help in sensing it? Is power over events largely the power of visualization, which few have developed?

Strategy Seventeen—*Altering*

Altering is an intervention that involves rearranging a specific part of a situation. Thus we can alter the setting, the dress, the goal, and so on. Whenever this occurs, it is through direct action and may involve pain. It may be somewhat shocking, in contrast to "shifting," which is a more gradual change.

Strategies Eighteen and Nineteen—*Redefining*

Redefining sounds like an intellectual process, but one can also redefine a problem, a feeling, or an experience. It is the kind of action that can occur only after a certain time. It resembles a reevaluation but is more definite. Many of Herbert Otto's methods, such as the life goals inquiry and the inventory of strengths, are designed to aid in redefining actions for purposes of future planning.[10]

Strategy Twenty—*Eliminating*

Eliminating may involve excreting or simply blotting out. It rids the system of something that is irrelevant or poisonous to healthy operation. In a different sense eliminating may be an experimental action involving the repression of a crucial variable such as a sensory channel. Such an action is not natural, but it helps to determine the importance of the function that has been temporarily eliminated.

As we review the preceding discussion of the actions suggested by the first twenty component strategies, some of which have been grouped together, several conclusions emerge. First, the direct analysis of specific strategies is in itself a useful and insightful process. Second, there appear to be clusters into which strategies can be grouped. For example, "spreading," "flowing," "nonresisting" and "least possible effort" appear to belong to one such cluster. It is unclear how many such clusters may exist or the extent to which they would account for the strategies listed. This can be determined only by a more systematic analysis, such as the one conducted in the following section. Third, we are left with a sense that identifying and analyzing component strategies is an action the effects of which are difficult to anticipate. We shift from a conviction of its fundamental importance, back to a tendency to pass it off as simply an unusual view of familiar material. It is not necessary to resolve this shifting picture. In fact, it would be premature to do so. But it is helpful to recognize its existence as a symptom of the particular phase of the discussion in which we are engaged.

The Extension of the Analysis

There are several approaches that can be taken to the analysis of the component strategies. Perhaps the most obvious is to attempt to arrange them into clusters. A subjective cluster analysis was conducted for this purpose. The groupings produced in this way are intended to be illustrative. A more systematic analysis would necessitate the clarification of categories, training of raters, and a more precise description of the strategies themselves.

Insofar as possible each strategy was placed in only one cluster, although there are several exceptions. Fourteen clusters were identified and described in this manner. They are described in terms of those strategies to which they seemed most clearly related. Each cluster is given in Appendix Four. In summary, the fourteen clusters are as follows:

1. Letting go.
2. Concretizing.
3. Variation of an element.
4. Communications.
5. Redistribution of energy.
6. Increasing personal involvement.
7. Manipulation.
8. Testing the limits.
9. Merging with a larger collectivity.
10. Controlling attention.
11. Problem solving.
12. Enhancement of creativity.
13. Self-image alteration.
14. Environmental alteration.

The Logical Generation of Additional Strategies

An obvious approach to collecting more strategies would be to continue the process by which the original list was compiled. This approach was not pursued because it had already demonstrated the outcome that could be expected, namely, more of the same.

After a period of trial and error several alternative approaches were developed. The first of these involved a more concentrated study of the nature of the key actions proposed in each of the strategies. For example, in strategy one the action is one of secreting; in strategy twelve, intervening; in strategy seventeen, one of altering. In each of these cases there is something one does that can be distinguished from its object or the setting in which it occurs. It takes the form of action which describes the crucial aspect of the strategy in the sense that it specifies what one must do. It seemed reasonable to direct some attention to these actions as a way of organizing and understanding more about the strategies themselves. To facilitate this task a list of actions was prepared from an inspection of the strategies. After the elimination of redundancies, the final version consisted of the actions listed in Appendix Five.

In each case we must assume that the action is being directed from someone or something to someone else or something else, all contained within a particular situation. Thus, when we consider the meaning of the fourth action "connecting," we must specify what is to be connected to what and under which general conditions. For example, is it the hand of one group member being connected to another in a darkened room or two apparently unrelated ideas being connected through a process of interpretation in a therapeutic session? The central action remains the same—bringing together things that were unrelated—but the strategies themselves are different. Each action may serve a host of different strategies.

From this point of view it is instructive to use Appendix Five as a means of relating strategies that seem quite different because of their objects but are revealed to share basic similar actions. For example, in the action of "reflecting," if one person physically reflects another, it is similar to the act of being a mirror, as used in theater games. If we mirror a person's ideas or feelings, the technique approaches the use of systematic feedback of the kind, "this is what I hear you saying or think you are feeling." The inner action of making visual photographs of oneself in action, as practiced in the Gurdieff work,[11] is a quite different use of reflecting in which one aspect of the individual reflects or is aware of what is happening in the other parts. Each of these strategies seems quite different because each has somewhat different objects and intentions, but the analysis suggests that this dissimilarity masks the underlying common core of the action they share. In this sense the emphasis on action rather than on object is helpful in relating approaches that seem different and in suggesting how the impact of a given action is transformed as its object or purpose is redefined.

A second general approach to the actions contained in Appendix Five is to group them into clusters as was done with the strategies from which they were derived. From such an effort one might evolve a typology of actions. Any given action could then be located within such a higher space configuration. This would have considerable advantage in attaining a parsimonious scientific description of the domain of actions covered by behavior change strategies.

A cursory inspection of Appendix Five indicates that such clustering of actions is possible. For example "free associating," "flowing," "emerging," "relaxing," "contacting," "allowing," "becoming," "moving," "fantasizing," and "pressing," "speaking," and "relating" all share a common core of meaning that might be described as "allowing," although each has a unique character of its own. Preliminary efforts at such a pattern analysis were encouraging, but the results tended to duplicate the clustering obtained using the strategies themselves.

Further inspection of these nouns suggested that in certain cases opposite actions were contained on the list—such as opening and closing or pushing and pulling. If in these cases opposite actions were listed, why not in all cases? Why if one listed "touching," could one not also list "not touching," or include "spontaneity" as the converse of "rehearsing beforehand." On the face of it each seemed to be a legitimate action under appropriate circumstances.

Several further examples may clarify the point. One can visualize a group situation in which one of the basic requirements is that the content of the group experience is secret, as in the traditional two-person therapy setting or the lawyer-client relationship. The converse of this arrangement is that nothing is privileged, which is precisely the condition that often exists in encounter groups, in which normal persons come together for mutual confrontation. Such activities are not defined as formally therapeutic and the imposition of secrecy is in some ways antithetical to the spirit of openness of communication that permeates the group's operation.

A second strategy, Number Seven, (See Appendix Three) involves forcing the issue by creating a situation that is so uncomfortable for the individual that he must act. The opposite of this strategy would be not to make the person do anything he does not want to do. This latter strategy is employed in nondirective approaches to counseling and is a feature of certain kinds of meditation that emphasize allowing experience to manifest itself in a natural manner.

An inversion of the strategy of making the common unique (Number 37), which is used in creativity training, would be to make the unique common. One example of such an approach is found in rational emotive therapy in which the patient is made to realize that something uniquely important to him that he fears (such as the loss of an important relationship), would not in fact be the end of the world. By separating the emotional reaction from the more logical aspects of the situation, the person is helped to see the relationship in a more sensible perspective.

These three examples suggest that the opposite of a

given strategy may also be a strategy in its own right although this does not necessarily hold for all strategies. However, it seems probable that it would hold for many of them which would greatly increase the range of alternatives available without further searching of the literature.

A second approach to action nouns is to hold the action constant and vary the focus or object of the action. For example, if we took the strategy of "forcing the issue," how would its effects vary if it were applied to thoughts, emotions, sensations, and physical actions?

There are numerous illustrations in the area of creative problem-solving that the refusal to drop a puzzling issue is a vital ingredient in achieving a creative breakthrough. In the emotional area the refusal to accept fear as a justification for avoiding an issue may be the prelude to entering an important area of therapeutic experience. In the area of personal sensations the utilization of pain can be an important means of controlling undesired behavior, as work in negative conditioning clearly suggests. Finally, in the realm of physical action, breaking out of a circle in which the individual must persist until he has successfully broken through a ring of other people appears to be a powerful method of mobilizing physical resources. Each of these outcomes is quite different, and the strategies with which they are identified are drawn from different areas and applied to different kinds of subjects. Nevertheless, the strategy used is identical in each case. Only the inter-personal object has been varied.

A Systematic Approach to the Generation of Strategies

The preceding analysis of the relation of a given strategy to different levels of human functioning suggests that there might be a number of such aspects to any strategy that could be systematically varied, both to generate new strategies and to clarify the generality of the given strategy.

A preliminary general description of such a set of categories was therefore evolved. The system is summarized in Table 2. The nature of the categories will be briefly described and illustrated. Although this classification scheme is tentative, it is sufficiently complex to illustrate the principles involved and the implications such an approach would have for the analysis of component strategies.

The first category involves the level of abstraction at which the strategy operates. If we speak of "letting go," this is a highly abstract concept, whereas if we say "become aware of how your left eye feels and let any unnecessary tension be released," this is a highly specific and concrete approach to the same general principle.

The second category concerns the point in time at which the strategy is typically utilized. Probably the majority of strategies are used during the mid-stages of the change process, but some are typically applied at the beginning or end. Others may be applied at any time, whereas still others are in a sense timeless. For example, the collection of relevant information about participants is usually done either before or after an experience. A microlab usually is utilized in the early phases of a group experience. Sensory awareness exercises may be utilized at any time, whereas meditation constitutes an attempt to contact the eternal moment that is within our normal concept of time as a flowing instant.

At the moment of its application each strategy has a common quality that can be characterized as pleasurable, painful, or neutral. "Allowing time for integration and relaxation," is usually a pleasurable experience. "Forcing the issue" is clearly unpleasant. "Splitting one's attention" is generally a neutral effort. These effects are not to be confused with the later results of the strategies. A painful strategy may often lead to a pleasant outcome.

Closely related to the quality of the experience is the nature of the effort required. There are two choices at any given moment: we can either let things happen or one can make things happen through conscious effort. When we relax by focusing on our heart beat, we allow something to come into awareness. However, when we ask an individual to express

Table 2—A Classification Scheme for Growth Strategies

1. Level of Abstraction
   a. high   b. medium   c. low

2. Location in Time Sequence
   a. pre-sequence
   b. beginning
   c. middle
   d. end
   e. post-sequence
   f. throughout
   g. outside of

3. Quality
   a. enjoyable
   b. neutral
   c. painful

4. Nature of Effort
   a. making it happen
   b. allowing it to happen

5. Direction
   a. out   b. in   c. two-way

6. Level of Effort
   a. intrapersonal
   b. interpersonal

7. Focus

Individual	Group	Environment
thought	popularity	
feeling	power	
sensing	composition	
moving	norms	
sex	roles	
self-awareness	task	
cosmic consciousness	communication network	

8. Purpose
   a. direct vs. indirect
   b. simple vs. complex
   c. immediate vs. enduring

9. Likelihood of Success
   a. little
   b. moderate
   c. great

10. Effect

his feelings to another person nonverbally, he must make a definite effort both to translate his feelings into action and to be willing to share his private emotions in the first place. Effort is often associated with pain and letting something happen is associated with pleasure, but this is not a perfect relationship. There are few things more terrifying than allowing oneself to experience a situation of which one is afraid.

Any strategy is directed from one person or object to another, or, in the limiting case, it is a two-way exchange. When a practitioner interprets a subject's behavior, the practitioner's action is directed from himself to the subject. When the subject freely associates, the direction of the action is reversed. When people are in the midst of a conversation about alternative paths to problem solution, the exchange is two-way.

There are two communications systems that may be involved in the application of any strategy—the intrapersonal and the interpersonal. If a person uses goal setting to plan his own future behavior, it is an intrapersonal action. If he sets the goals for another person's behavior, the action is interpersonal; all other aspects of the action are constant. Conceptually, it is possible to subdivide interpersonal action into dyadic, group, organizational, and cultural action. Each succeeding unit includes the others. For present purposes it was considered sufficient to utilize a simple binary distinction between inside and outside the individual, without further extension of the analysis.

The foci of the change effort are an important and relatively complex category. These foci fall into two broad categories—individual and group. The individual cluster includes thought, feeling, sensing, moving, sex, self-awareness, and cosmic consciousness. Of these, the last three require some comment.

It may seem strange that sex is not simply classified as a joint product of sensing, moving, and feeling. Such a position is certainly tenable. But the pervasiveness of sex as an unconscious determinant of human behavior suggests that it may be valuable to consider it separately.

Self-awareness is separately considered because it is not necessary for us to be aware of ourselves in order to think, feel, sense, move, and make love. These things can happen with relatively little awareness. To become aware of doing something while doing it requires a special kind of effort. How many readers, for example, are aware of themselves as a body in space with eyes engaged in reading a page that is in front of them in a certain room at this given moment? It is not necessary to feel one's body in space in order to read. That is an additional aspect of the situation.

Cosmic awareness differs from self-awareness in that it goes beyond being present at the moment and provides an experience of contact with the universe that differs from the one usually presented to the senses. We mean here not fantasy and hallucination induced through drugs, fasts, and other unusual or extreme conditions, but a new way of perceiving the world and one's relation to it. Such perception is widely documented in religious literature. Our intention is not to validate such experiences, but rather to allow a place for them in our conceptual system since some of the strategies that we are analyzing have this form of consciousness as their eventual objective.

The categories listed under "group" include popularity, status, power distribution, composition, norms, roles, tasks and communication network. This list is by no means exhaustive, but it does include some major aspects of group functioning which, although requiring individuals for their concrete manifestation, are unique group phenomena. A final "environment" category involves physical and social influences of a more general character.

The *purpose* of a strategy can be classified in terms of three categories. First, it is either direct or indirect. Second, it is simple or complex. Third, it is limited or more enduring. If one is asked to stretch one's arms over one's head as a means of relaxing the shoulder muscles, the purpose might be classified as indirect (relaxation is attained by stretching against tight muscles), simple (one is attempting to do only one thing), and limited (there is no assumption that the resulting relaxation will last for any length of time).

One of the most difficult categories to utilize reliably is the likelihood of success that the given strategy possesses. Nevertheless, different strategies may share the same objective with different degrees of likelihood in attaining it. For example, reinforcement of a desired behavior may produce the same effect as creating an insight within the individual through interpretation. The relative effectiveness of these alternates must be weighed along with other factors such as their practicality and ease, the special conditions required, the nature of the subjects, and so on. There is also probably an inverse relationship between likelihood of success and importance of the change. Those methods that work best do so on changes that are less important or desirable. To the extent that this is the case, we must sometimes choose between methods that may not work but are attempting to produce powerful change, and those that are more successful but whose effects are relatively trivial.

Finally, it is necessary to specify what effects the strategy is intended to produce. Here no effort is made to break down the alternatives into categories. The usual nature of the effect is the dependent variable in the situation. It may vary with the needs of the individual, the change agent, or other more general requirements of society. The same strategy may be used to create different effects (e.g., touching may be used for support, communication, or sensing), and different strategies may have the same effect. Although it may be possible to analyze these effects into more general groupings after further studies of strategies, this is a premature issue at present. Suffice it to say that they all come under the general heading of improving the positive functioning of the individual or the group either directly or indirectly by removing some inhibiting influence.

In summary, the categories listed in Table 2 are illustrative of the kind of comprehensive system that can be developed for describing any component strategy in general terms.

Such a system can aid in making a systematic classification of strategies, but this is only its most pedestrian use. The major purpose for which it was devised was not to describe strategies already identified, but to aid in the identification of new ones without having to search the behavior change literature in ever widening circles. How this can be done can be illustrated by taking a particular strategy, showing how it would be classified, and analyzing how shifting its classification would alter its nature and impact. Technically, this approach is known as a sensitivity analysis.

To illustrate this process Strategy 155 was selected, mainly because of its simplicity and clarity. This strategy consists in referring to a person by his last name only, i.e., Mr. Jones, or Mrs. Smith. It is employed in the work developed by Gurdjieff and Uspenski as a small means of fostering individual growth.[11] The purpose of the exercise is to remind the individual that his social self (the Mr. Jones who is being addressed) is not his real one; instead it is a construct produced through social influence. In terms of the conceptual scheme we have been outlining this strategy could be described as follows: Its level of abstraction is low; it can be applied throughout the time sequence; its quality is neutral; the nature of effort required is one of making it happen; it is used by a group of people so that its direction is two-way; the level of effort is interpersonal; the focus is on the role definition of the individual; it is direct, simple, and immediate; its likelihood of success is moderate; and its effect is to help the person to remember his true self and not be identified with his socially created personality.

For purposes of a sensitivity analysis here each of these categories will be shifted one at a time and the impact of this alteration on the effect of the strategy will be discussed.

From concrete to abstract: In order to redefine the strategy into a more abstract form one person might say to another periodically "remember who you really are," instead of addressing him as "Mr. Smith." This procedure could have several effects. It might eliminate the formality associated with calling someone Mr. or Mrs. all the time and indirectly show a more personal concern for the individual. Further, it would tend to become more awkward over time, whereas one can call someone else Mr. X more or less indefinitely.

Shift in time sequence: If an individual were referred to as Mr. X only in the beginning of a situation, it might have the effect of helping him to start the action in an effective way without the danger of the strategy's becoming hackneyed through overuse, provided that this form of address were associated in his mind with the goals of the action. If it were employed in the middle of the situation, it might keep him from getting lost just at the time when most work turns into routine. If used at the end, it might help him to reorient himself to his original purpose and perhaps help him to attain a second wind. When used either before or after a given situation, it might help the individual to attain the proper detachment necessary for an effective planning or evaluation of the situation. Finally, if a person were called Mr. Smith only at moments when he was not acting from his personality, such as when in meditation, it might increase the depth of such experience by providing outside feedback of an objective nature that reinforced the fact that he was in fact in a better state.

Quality: The strategy might be made painful if it were employed only when the individual was acting in an unconscious, mechanical manner. It would then take on the character of a reprimand. Conversely, if the strategy were employed when the individual was acting with sensitivity, awareness, and effectiveness, it would have the character of a verbal reward. Each of these variations would turn the strategy into a conditioning procedure.

Nature of effort: If the individual attempted to accept himself as he was whenever he was addressed as Mr. X, the effect of the strategy would be changed, from making him discriminate between the false from the real to one of accepting of the actual.

Direction: If the strategy were directed from the individual to others only, the individual would be taking the role of a teacher who must act with awareness to help other persons.

If the individual is exclusively on the receiving end of the strategy, he is in the student's role, receiving help from others.

Level of effort: If one referred to oneself as Mr. X either in public or private, rather than being referred to in this way by others, it would act as a distancing strategy, give one perspective on one's own actions and minimize one's identification with them.

Focus: If each of the individual's functions were referred to as Mr. X's rather than as "mine," they would be viewed with greater objectivity and detachment. With the group elements the outcome is more varied and complex. In terms of "popularity," one might use Mr. X as a term indicating that one liked the particular person involved. In terms of "power," the use of a Mr. X form of address for all persons would have a leveling effect by making everyone equal. The effect on group composition of the Mr. X strategy depends on the variable of familiarity. The better the group members know one another from previous experience, the greater the impact of the Mr. X strategy is likely to be because the formality would be unexpected. If the use of last names only is part of the norm, it will tend to have less effect than if it is not. The more that it deviates from that which would occur according to social custom, the greater the shock it provides and the less likely there is to be ambiguity associated with its use. In terms of "task," one might use the Mr. X strategy when working and revert to first names when socializing. This pattern of utilization would help to clarify the differences between the situations and serve as a subtle form of reinforcing the correct and appropriate action in each instance. Finally, in terms of the "communications network," one might employ the Mr. X strategy when initiating communication with an individual and thereafter use first names. In this way the conversation would begin with a reminder that the real rather than the social person should function and also add to the awareness of the communicator that he was in fact initiating a new sequence of action.

Purpose: In order to make the purpose indirect one

might ask the person to recall each time Mr. X was referred to when he had last been addressed as Mr. X and check with other persons if this were accurate. In this way the actual use of Mr. X is only a means to an end of testing the awareness of the individual. In order to make the strategy complex, one might require the individual to recall what he was doing each time he had been called Mr. X, since the last time the term was used. In this way the strategy is not only a reminder but an initiator of a recollection process. Finally, in order to make the strategy more enduring in its effect, we might use post-hypnotic suggestion to increase the impact on the individual of the use of the strategy. He could be instructed under hypnosis to have a deep insight into his own character when the phrase was used. Similar intensification of effect might be produced by conditioning or visualization procedures used in conjunction with the basic strategy.

Likelihood of success: The impact of the strategy might be increased if it were used as a reward immediately after a positive action. The likelihood of success would be decreased if the individual is expected to make an effort at self-remembering strictly on his own every time the phrase Mr. X is used in relation to him.

In summarizing the preceding discussion several implications can be drawn. First, the process of generating strategies seems more subtle than was at first apparent. Slight variations in descriptive category can change the strategy's effect clearly. This was well illustrated by the shift from concrete to abstract emphasis in the utilization of the Mr. X strategy, which altered not only the formality of the change effort but appeared to increase its immediate impact.

Second, the utilization of a classification scheme for purposes of developing new strategies enables us to estimate how many such strategies there may be. Thus, if there are three levels of abstraction, seven locations in time sequence, three levels of quality, two kinds of effort, three directions of effort, two levels of effort, fifteen foci, three purposes, and three degrees of likelihood of success associated with any strategy, a total of forty-one single variations are possible for any given strategy. Some of the logical differences may not represent meaningful differences. Nevertheless, the implication is clear that we are dealing with a vast array of possibilities.

Third, utilizing a sensitivity analysis approach to any strategy helps us to understand something about its essential nature that may not be apparent in the form in which it appears in the literature. In the illustration employed above a basic aspect of the strategy was the utilization of secret signals to indicate to the individual special information that an outsider would not understand. This aspect of the strategy was less clear in its original form than in many of the variations derived from it.

Fourth, there may be effects of categories that are generalized over strategies. For example, variation in the quality of the experience from pleasurable to painful may have certain typical effects regardless of the strategy in which the variation occurs. Or use at the beginning rather than the end of an experience may have certain systematic effects on the strategy that are independent of its particular form.

Fifth, the utilization of a conceptual scheme, by permitting the specification of all logical possibilities, makes it possible to uncover ways of working that have not occurred to practitioners. It offers a systematic way of generating new strategies that is unbiased by historical, cultural, or stylistic influences that generally exert a strong influence on the development of new techniques.

Beyond all these specific points, which are based on considering each category used to describe the strategy separately, is the array of possibilities that can be generated by changing two or more categories at a time. Further, one must consider the effect of using more than one strategy within the same context. Such a synthetic approach to the generation of methods opens up a vast realm that is as alarming in its magnitude as it is challenging in its possibilities. On the other hand, it represents a close approximation to normal social behavior, which does in fact consist of series of strategies employed in a specified order. It is only as such orderings are first broken down and then resynthesized that any understanding and control can be attained in this area.

The Automation of Behavior Change

At this point we have at our disposal a bewildering array of alternative actions. How are we to choose between them at any given moment, and how are they to be related to a realistic continuous growth process?

These questions are far easier to ask than to answer. One method of asking and answering simultaneously is to attempt to build a model of the change process. Any such model should be as simple as possible but also sufficiently general to adapt to the variety of strategies at our disposal.

Several basic assumptions held by behavioral scientists of various persuasions will be employed. First, any individual, group, or situation that is the focus of change is normally in a homeostatic condition, i.e., it represents a dynamically balanced system. The roles, norms, goals, habit patterns, and environmental influences that are related to the particular situation are formed to facilitate this general condition. This is their basic underlying function.

Second, it must be possible for the situation to be improved. Unless this assumption is tenable, there is no justification for a change attempt. The amount of improvement possible may differ as may relative importance in terms of conflicting alternatives that compete for limited resources.

Third, the practitioner involved in the situation can be viewed as performing a catalytic function. It is his purpose to create or facilitate constructive change without himself necessarily being altered. If he is affected, it is an incidental benefit.

Fourth, the practitioner does not act until external evidence makes it appear that such action is appropriate. He does not destroy a relatively satisfactory equilibrium simply because in his view things could and should be better. He functions only when objective signs of disequilibrium appear.

Fifth, any strategy the practitioner employs has as its essential function the re-establishment of the equilibrium of the system at a higher level of productivity and contentment than it had before his action.

In order to suggest how these assumptions relate to actual behavior, a specific example is helpful: A group is meeting in the home of one of its members for the first time. The leader asks the group how they feel about the new setting. Various innocuous answers are given. Finally Mike says, "I don't feel free to say what I really think." (This statement suggests a potential imbalance in the state of the group. If Mike allowed himself to be frank, he would upset his relationship with Ann in whose house they are meeting.) The leader says to Ann, "Do you mind if Mike says what he really thinks?" Ann says "No. You should tell the truth." (In this manner Mike is reassured, before the fact, that any disturbance he creates will be accepted, if not appreciated.) "Before you begin," the leader says, "I would like to have you both sit in the middle of the group and hold hands." (This procedure is designed to intensify the encounter. Further, by making physical contact Mike is given an added communications channel to help understand how Ann is reacting to what he says. This strategy also has the effect of rewarding Mike by giving him the enjoyment of physical contact before the fact of saying something unpleasant.) Mike then begins to talk. "You know, Ann, at this point I don't have anything so terrible to say about your house. What I am more interested in is you. I want to get to know you better. But your talk about your boy friend last week slowed me up."

"I am here now," says Ann.

They talk together for about five minutes sharing their feelings about one another. Finally they pause. There is a silence as they realize that they are not alone. The group has been watching them.

"Did you forget all about the group?" asks the leader.

"Yes. I guess I knew they were there somewhere, but I wasn't aware of them."

"How about you, Ann?"

"I forgot about them, too."

This absorption in their relationship suggests that for Mike and Ann a new equilibrium, marked by greater intimacy and sharing, has been achieved. However, in the course of this action they had psychologically removed themselves from the group. This source of imbalance needs to be corrected.

"How did some of the rest of you feel about what was happening?" asks the leader in order to start initial communication between Mike and Ann and the remaining group members. Slowly group members give their comments about their personal views of Mike and Ann and how they themselves are feeling. In the end Mike and Ann are related to the rest of the group and the various imbalances produced by the initial remark of Mike's about telling what he really feels have been handled through a variety of simple strategies on the leader's part.

How does the preceding relate to possible automation of such processes? To answer this question it is necessary provisionally to accept the assumptions that have been made about the change process. We must also assume that alternative change strategies are stored in an appropriate location—either the memory of a computer or that of the practitioner. If this is the case, we can visualize the practitioner as performing a crucial link in a man-machine interaction. The machine (computer or brain) contains in its memory a listing of strategies, their nature, limitations, and effects. The practitioner performs the diagnostic function of identifying the source of disequilibrium at a given moment, and such other features of the immediate situation as may be relevant for decision making, and feeds these to the computer. On the basis of this information the machine suggests alternative strategies as the basis for action. The value of such a process is directly proportional to the amount of information available about each strategy. Its advantage is that it is systematic, comprehensive, and objective.

But is it realistic to assume that system disfunctions are readily discernible? Generally they are. One of the criteria of social competence is, in fact, the ability to recognize such signs and act accordingly, because they represent signals of coming difficulty or promises of possible opportunities for a better state.

This orientation to system imbalance helps us to redefine the utilization of behavioral strategies themselves. What we need to know is how specific strategies will affect specific types of system disturbances. For example, if a goal conflict exists in a system between personal enhancement and group productivity, what will be the relative effects of a letting go versus a testing-the-limits strategy? Letting go may reduce the conflict but lead to consequences that the individual is unwilling to accept in the long run. Testing the limits may intensify the conflict by forcing a choice. These alternatives are of practical as well as theoretical importance. This kind of examination of the implications of alternative strategies to specific system imbalances requires further development. Any given strategy is not equally effective with every kind of imbalance, whatever the general level of its potency. The classification of strategies by their effect on a specific type of situational imbalance provides a means of interpreting their effects that has been lacking to this point. The previous efforts were directed toward generating new strategies from the information uncovered in the search of old ones. The present model offers a tentative suggestion for organizing these strategies for use, whether automated or not, on a level of action appropriate to their nature.

Research on Component Strategies

The traditional pattern of evaluation research involves the comparison of an experimental and a control group on specific change criteria. The groups are matched with the exception of the change procedure, which is administered to the experimental group.

There are countless studies that fit this general format in the professional literature. In general, these studies have not been fruitful in proportion to the work involved for a variety of technical and social psychological reasons. These difficulties have been dealt with in detail elsewhere but will be briefly summarized here for purposes of laying the foundation for the present discussion.[12]

The technical issues involved include measuring the effect of the change method, the influence of the practitioner, the effect of the subjects, and the control of the experimental method. Any effort to detect change must utilize measuring instruments. No matter how carefully developed, these instruments are open to various forms of bias. Subjects may give socially desirable answers rather than expressing how they actually feel. Practitioners may unconsciously coach subjects in the "correct" answers, so that the change that is produced by the subjects is no more than their learning how the practitioner wants them to respond to the test instruments. A further technical problem concerns measurement-method interaction. Certain instruments used to measure given methods may increase the effectiveness of the method, by sensitizing the subjects to the kind of change being measured or reinforcing certain aspects of the change experience itself.

A second major difficulty is separating the effect of the practitioner from that of the method he uses. More specifically one must distinguish between the impact of the practitioner's personality, his degree of expertise, and the impact of his own belief system. All these factors may produce change that must be distinguished from change produced by the particular method he is employing.

A third source of confusion is related to the subjects under investigation. One must distinguish between the effect of the special attention given to subjects in the experimental group and the nature of that attention. The faith of the subjects in either the practitioner or the method that he uses is also a potent influence that must be separated from the change owing to the method, regardless of the degree of faith the subjects have in it.

A final major source of technical difficulty involves the control of the method being evaluated. One of the traditional requirements of experimental technique is that the treatment must be reproducible. In most evaluation studies the methods used are almost impossible to describe with sufficient precision to reproduce them faithfully. A related problem is that experimenters often fail to prove that they are studying the methods they think they are studying. This may seem like a picayune point, but one cannot take for granted that practitioners actually do what they say in print that they do.

Beyond all these technical problems that confront the evaluation of behavior change methods is a series of social difficulties that arise if such research is conducted under field conditions within institutional settings. These include the control of communications channels, the relationship between researcher and practitioner, the number of practitioners utilized, the effect of a control group, the effect of the study on the change process, and the utilization of the findings.

From the viewpoint of the researcher it is desirable to keep information about the subjects who are involved in the study as isolated as possible from other persons within a given organization or institution, so that the subjects' experience will not be contaminated by the actions and attitudes of persons not directly involved in the study. This need runs directly counter to the requirement for free access to information necessary for the efficient functioning of the institution.

The researcher is in a privileged position in comparison to the practitioner whom he evaluates. He does not have a case load and is not burdened with many of the administrative procedures to which any practitioner working within an organization has to conform. His hours are not closely supervised, for example. These differences can lead to misunderstanding, envy, and distrust unless the researcher makes special efforts to overcome this potential source of misunderstanding.

Further, the researcher would rather have a number of practitioners involved in the research to lend generality to his results. However, from the point of view of the institution, shifting and turnover of personnel are extremely undesirable. The use of a control group, which is essential in evaluation research, creates certain ethical dilemmas. Persons who might benefit are deprived of treatment because of scientific requirements. The necessity for this kind of sacrifice has become widely accepted, but the dilemma remains.

The conduct of evaluation within an organization has many unexpected effects, which administrators often do not anticipate. Hence, an evaluation may be threatening. Practitioners have little to gain and much to lose. Further, in the course of data gathering, facts about institutional functioning may be brought to light that could lead to general embarrassment and go beyond the confines of the particular method under evaluation. Thus enthusiasm wanes as research progresses, and the climate required for accepting and utilizing findings is undermined.

It is customary to evaluate new, rather than standard, procedures. This means that what is evaluated is in a preliminary state, not in the mature and reliable form that it will take after suitable testing on the job. The results of such an evaluation may well be irrelevant, whether they are positive or negative.

Finally, the length of time required to conduct evaluative research (often three to five years) may mean that related administrative decisions must be made before the results of the research are available.

All of the foregoing discussion suggests the difficulty of conducting effective evaluation research. However, even when such difficulties have been overcome, a much broader problem remains: Such research provides the kind of answer that has relatively little scientific interest. Specifically, it determines whether a given complex procedure, which is impossible to describe precisely, has any demonstrable effect. If it does, one still cannot tell why. Is it the skill of the practitioner, the faith of the subject, the unintended effect of the measuring instrument, the special attention received by the experimental group, and so on, or is it the method itself? Although there are procedures designed to eliminate many of these possibilities, they involve much added labor and sophistication of design. At the end of such an effort one is really little better off scientifically than one was before. The main justification for such a study is administrative decision making, but as already pointed out, such decisions are often made before the studies are completed.

How does the study of component strategies compare in ease and effectiveness with ordinary evaluation research on complex procedures? Does it involve the same technical and social psychological complexities? Does it provide the same basic ambiguity of final result? To answer these basic questions it is helpful to describe how such research might be conducted and then relate this example to the problems previously described.

The model to be employed in this design has several important features. First, a number of different strategies are evaluated within the same study. Second, the study is performed under controlled laboratory conditions. Third, the design is such as to permit the utilization of multivariate statistical analysis.

For purposes of this illustration let us select three different kinds of strategies: variation in feedback, alternation of power structure, and stress. Each of these can be subdivided. To take some account of these gradations and differences, four forms of feedback, three types of power structure, and three degrees of stress are utilized—objective, subjective, and positive and negative feedback; laissez-faire, democratic, and autocratic power; high, medium, and low stress.

When each of these conditions is combined three at a time there will be $4 \times 3 \times 3$ or thirty-six different treatment conditions to be evaluated. Each of these conditions consists of a unique combination of the three types of strategies. Thus, one condition might consist of low stress, subjective feedback, and laissez-faire power structure, whereas another might consist of high stress, positive feedback, and authoritarian power structure. The various possibilities are indicated in Table 3.

If we started with 180 subjects, we could randomly assign them each to one of the thirty-six conditions, so that

Table 3—The Thirty-six Experimental Conditions

1.	1	5	8	19.	3	5	8
2.	1	6	8	20.	3	6	8
3.	1	7	8	21.	3	7	8
4.	1	5	9	22.	3	5	9
5.	1	5	10	23.	3	5	10
6.	1	6	9	24.	3	6	9
7.	1	6	10	25.	3	6	10
8.	1	7	9	26.	3	7	9
9.	1	7	10	27.	3	7	10
10.	2	5	8	28.	4	5	8
11.	2	6	8	29.	4	6	8
12.	2	7	8	30.	4	7	8
13.	2	5	9	31.	4	5	9
14.	2	5	10	32.	4	5	10
15.	2	6	9	33.	4	6	9
16.	2	6	10	34.	4	6	10
17.	2	7	9	35.	4	7	9
18.	2	7	10	36.	4	7	10

KEY

1—subjective feedback
2—objective feedback
3—positive feedback
4—negative feedback

5—authoritarian power structure
6—democratic power structure
7—laissez-faire power structure

8—low stress
9—medium stress
10—high stress

each condition would be experienced by five people. This might seem like an ambitious undertaking, but it would be premature to draw such a conclusion until the output of this study is described.

Although each of the thirty-six treatments is different, they would be evaluated in terms of a common set of change measures. These might involve a measure of participation, social popularity, personality characteristics, achievement motivation, and the like. The main criteria for such measures is that they should be relevant to the strategies, sensitive to change, and relatively easy to administer. Such measures might be applied before and after experimental experience or post only.

In order to visualize this process more clearly it is helpful to describe the nature of two of the experimental conditions. For example, condition number 14 consists of authoritarian power structure, objective feedback, and high stress. This condition might be approximated using the following procedure. Five randomly assigned subjects are placed in a room utilized for testing purposes. They are given a standard set of tasks employing a variety of different problem-solving and human relations skills. These tasks constitute both an activity and a testing device. An autocratic leader is randomly selected from the five group members. The group is informed that he is the leader and that failure to follow his direction will be punished. Further, lack of productivity will also be punished. This punishment will consist of a moderately disagreeable but harmless electric shock that can be administered at will by the experimenter who is placed behind a one-way mirror. Half-way through the testing period objective feedback is provided through videotape playback. This procedure is designed to provide autocratic leadership, high stress, and objective feedback conditions while leaving other variables standardized.

A contrasting condition, number 3, would consist of laissez-faire power structure, low stress, and subjective feedback. In this instance the group members would be admitted to the testing room, shown the materials required for the tasks, and told that they were free to do whatever they wanted to do. Half-way through the testing period a tape recording of a standardized subjective feedback would be played to them. Such a recording would have to be pretested to ensure its general relevance to the kind of situation to which it would be applied. If this proves impractical, an experimenter would observe the group and give his own subjective reactions. It is preferable to standardize the feedback, however, so that all groups having subjective feedback receive the same information.

In each of the other thirty-four treatments a similar formulation of the nature of the group experience would have to be made. This would require some thought and pretesting to make sure the instructions correspond to the intent of what was supposed to be tested.

Although this sounds like an imposing amount of work, it is in reality not a great deal more than is necessary in any multivariate experimental study. Many studies involving behavior change involve 100 or more subjects. Often each subject must be separately studied, whereas in the present design they can be handled five at a time. Most change studies utilize multiple criteria and many evaluation studies of complex methods require extensive subject exposure over months and years involving far greater investment of both subject and scientific time.

The crucial question, however, is what information such a study would provide. There are three kinds of questions which the data from this study can answer.

The first question is whether a given strategy produces any effect. For example, in relation to stress we might ask whether variations in stress have a direct or curvilinear influence, and if so, on which kinds of change criteria? In terms of feedback the situation is more complex. We are dealing with two dimensions of feedback within one design subjective-objective and positive-negative. Thus, we can compare one dimension with another, or each of the four kinds of feedback to one another. Power relations seem to fall on a natural scale ranging from laissez-faire through democratic and ending in autocratic. As with stress we can examine whether the relation is curvilinear (i.e., whether democracy, in the middle of the scale, has a greater impact than either extreme) or linear.

Not only is it possible to compare these variations of a given strategy, but it is further possible to compare the relative effectiveness of the three strategies to one another. Is stress a more potent change producer than power structure? Is feedback more effective in general than power structure, and so on? This kind of comparative analysis is precisely the kind of information that decision makers require when making selections between alternate strategies and is therefore of particular practical importance.

The second major source of information provided by an analysis of the data concerns the interaction between strategies. Here we have three possibilities. Is there an interaction (a) between feedback and power; (b) between feedback and stress, and (c) between stress and power? "Interaction" refers to the possibility that two variables acting jointly have a greater impact than knowledge of their separate effects would lead one to expect. This kind of information highlights combinations of particular potency. It is hard to overestimate the usefulness of detecting such interactions where they exist, in order to combine strategies that have the greatest possible effectiveness.

The third major source of information concerns the joint effect of the particular combinations of power, feedback, and stress that characterize a particular experimental condition. There are thirty-six such conditions. What is their relative effectiveness in terms of the change criteria? Does a condition of autocratic, high stress objective feedback, for example, produce more change than democratic, positive feedback and medium stress? The importance of this information is that the experimental treatment is in many cases an experimental analogue of existing approaches to social influence, so that in determining the effect of the particular conditions one learns something about methods that were not directly tested. To illustrate the possibilities of such an analysis let us briefly relate five of the experimental conditions to the methods to which they seem to correspond. These particular treatments are not selected to prove a point but are chosen more or less at random from the list given in Table 3.

For example, consider the case of an authoritarian power structure with objective feedback and high stress. Such a condition resembles certain kinds of staff meetings that occur in large corporate enterprises. The complementary situation is one of laissez-faire structure, subjective feedback, and low stress. This condition resembles a friendly social gathering such as a dinner or cocktail party. A third alternative is a democratic structure with positive feedback and moderate stress. This condition is found in certain types of volunteer action groups. A related condition is one of laissez-faire structure with positive feedback and low stress. This would resemble the nondirective approach in psychotherapy in which the therapist does not tell the patient what to do but provides constant interest and encouragement. A final example is authoritarian structure with negative feedback and high stress. This situation is characteristic of the earlier phases of brain washing. The captive is at the mercy of the interrogator. Whatever he does is wrong, and the penalty for being wrong is very high.

It seems reasonable to conclude from these examples that many of the possible combinations of strategies have interesting and important analogues in social reality. To the extent that this is the case, one is learning something about the effectiveness of these other approaches by such a laboratory study, even though we have not fully recreated any of them. Further, we are studying these broadly different experiences within a comparative framework so that their efficacy in producing change on given criteria can be directly compared with one another.

To obtain all the foregoing information from the data provided by this kind of study, the basic statistical analysis would involve a three-way analysis of variance. This would answer the questions relating to main effects and interactions. The third question involving the comparison of experimental conditions can be answered by statistics that are designed to test multiple comparisons of the experimental cells, such as that devised by Tukey.[13]

For the behavioral scientist all the preceding fits a well-established pattern. It combines the experimental approach with sophisticated multivariate statistical analysis to obtain a relatively great amount of information from the smallest possible effort. This example is not the only approach, but it is one that seems to be relevant, practical, and powerful.

Before concluding this section, it will be helpful to compare the difficulties associated with ordinary evaluation research of whole methods, as previously described, with the above multivariate experimental procedures. As already indicated, these difficulties are of two major types—technical and social. In general it can be said that the study of strategies eliminates all the social difficulties that arise when a complex behavior change method is evaluated in a naturalistic setting because strategies can be studied under laboratory conditions, which by definition do not incur these difficulties.

In regard to the technical problems associated with evaluation research, the study of strategies either eliminates or simplifies them. Specifically in relation to instruments used to measure change, there is less likelihood for bias to enter. All subjects have had some kind of treatment, and the preference of the experimenter or his agents for any particular treatment is minimized because no known method is being directly evaluated. The impact of the practitioner's personality, experience, and belief system is also minimized because of the specificity of the instructions in each experimental condition, which minimize the role played by the practitioner. Similarly, the belief systems of the subjects have little influence because they do not have previous knowledge about the particular method they are to receive. So far as they and the experimenter are concerned, all treatments may be effective, and therefore the influence of faith is either minimized or spread throughout the design.

Finally, and of greatest importance, the study of strategies in the multivariate design outlined above eliminates the inherent ambiguity of all evaluation research. A known strategy or set of strategies is evaluated under conditions that can be duplicated or replicated. This situation can rarely if ever be satisfied by ordinary evaluation studies of known methods in naturalistic settings.

In summary, we have suggested that the study of whole methods as ordinarily undertaken in traditional evaluative research is a difficult undertaking that provides information of dubious value even to the practitioner. In contrast, the study of strategies in the design that has been illustrated provides the possibility of a wealth of reliable information that is not unduly difficult to obtain, and most important, can be built upon cumulatively by subsequent investigations.

THE BEHAVIOR CHANGE
METHODS IN THE SAMPLE

1. Psychosynthesis, Catharsis Methods
2. Psychosynthesis, Critical Analysis Method
3. Client-Centered Therapy
4. T-Groups
5. Focusing (E. T. Gendlin)
6. Human Potential Groups (H. A. Otto)
7. Symbo Experiment (H. Maupin)
8. Self-Directed Groups
9. Psychodrama
10. Gestalt Therapy
11. Synectics (Gorden)
12. Improvisational Theater (V. Spolin)
13. Progressive Relaxation (E. Jacobson)
14. Tai Chi Chuan
15. Movement in Depth (M. Whitehouse)
16. Eurythmy (E. Dalcroze)
17. Sensory Awareness (C. Selver)
18. Sensory Massage (B. Gunther)
19. Bioenergetic Analysis
20. Autogenic Training
21. Oriental Martial Arts (Judo, Karate, Aikido)
22. Structural Integration (I. Rolf)
23. National Training School for Boys (I. Golddiamond)
24. Psychosynthesis, Will Methods
25. Mental Health Through Will Training (Recovery Inc.)

94. Relaxation through progressive removal of tension from specific muscle groups.
95. Relaxation through directing attention around the body.
96. Relaxation through entering organic rhythms.
97. Relaxation as prelude to greater internal or external contact.
98. Heightening of imagery flow: (a) giving a specific image as a starting point, (b) focusing on element in free flow of associations, (c) giving a spatial orientation as start of imagery, (d) identifying with a general organic process such as a growing seed.
99. Utilization of creative experience as a reward to help individual face painful situations.
100. Utilization of external rewards (e.g., love, acceptance) to facilitate painful confrontations.
101. Expanding one's definition of reality.
102. Focusing on a supra-individual entity.
103. Sharing experience for mutual comfort.
104. Suspension of basic assumptions about reality.
105. Sensing the physical basis for all action. Being aware of the physical background, orientation and location for each thought, emotion and movement.
106. Remembering oneself in the midst of action.
107. Use of direct suggestion to change originating: (a) from self, (b) from other.
108. Use of analogies for training creativity.
109. Silence.
110. Relegation of authority from self to other.
111. Focusing on the avoided: (a) content, (b) affect.
112. Testing the limits.
113. Consciously acting a given role in a nontheatrical situation.
114. Setting a goal.
115. Objectifying subjective determinants of world view.
116. Attending not to what is said, but what is not said.
117. Changing one's name.
118. Contacting experience of which one was unaware.
119. Coaching.
120. Listening.
121. Establishing point of concentration.
122. Performing a ritual action.
123. Allowing the situation to remain unresolved.
124. Brainstorming.
125. Changing physiological state through: (a) breathing, (b) rhythmic actions, (c) fasting, (d) mortification, (e) drugs and chemicals.
126. Sensing space.
127. Moving to music spontaneously and expressively.
128. Encountering another nonverbally.
129. Describing one's first impression.

130. Having a group fantasy.
131. Expressing physical aggression.
132. Providing a positive strength bombardment.
133. Breathing in a conscious rhythm.
134. Use of breath as focus of meditation.
135. Transformation of negative energy to muscular energy.
136. Use of sensory cues within visualization to increase depth of involvement: e.g., temperature, taste, smell, heart beat.
137. Conscious expression of negative emotion.
138. Rapidly performing a number of different kinds of acts.
139. Becoming aware of how one feels when taking the basic physical postures of sitting, lying, and standing.
140. Enacting different types of physical actions, e.g., swinging, turning, opening, and closing, folding and unfolding.
141. Letting the environment "talk" to the individual.
142. Repeatedly returning to a problem.
143. Use of imagery to aid problem solving.
144. Switching from one strategy to another.
145. Making a personal inventory.
146. Undoing Karma by reliving old situation in a new way.
147. Use of imaginal deconditioning.
148. Going through physical reorienting process after an intense fantasy.
149. Playing games.
150. Conducting multiple conversations.
151. Moving in and out of two independent situations occurring simultaneously.
152. Creating an unstable situation.
153. Mismatching of persons in a group.
154. Mismatching of persons to tasks.
155. Referring to individual by last name only (e.g., Mr. K).
156. Relating specific motions, emotions, thoughts, and sensations to each other.
157. Doing a task while focusing on a specific sensation.
158. Taking mental photographs of how one appears from the outside.
159. Performing unfamiliar roles.
160. Reading sacred scripture.
161. Going through stages of initiation.
162. Creating a shock by inappropriate behavior.
163. Performing physical work.
164. Use of periodic shocks to maintain motivation.
165. Making a payment for services.
166. Consciously suffering pain in order to grow.
167. Giving to another only what he asks for.
168. Making a public commitment.
169. Keeping a situation in constant motion.
170. Slowing down normal functions.

171. Separation of sexes for given activity.
172. Emphasizing the normative.
173. Emphasizing variation.
174. Shifting from one emotion to another.
175. Surrendering the illusion of personal unity created through possessing one body and one name.
176. Accepting nothing.
177. Attending inward.
178. Having a clearly defined aim.
179. Making an effort.
180. Not identifying with favorite negative emotion.
181. Going against one's natural tendency or the expectations of others.
182. Learning about self from watching one's reaction to others.
183. Passing on what one has received.
184. Playing any part required by external conditions.
185. Putting things together that are not ordinarily related.
186. Portraying one's inner world.
187. Portraying a role in a given social situation.
188. Communicating with different selves.
189. Generating an emotion that one does not initially feel.
190. Communicating with others as if one were talking to one's self.
191. Associating memories to given stimuli.
192. Becoming aware that we are the cause of our own physical tension.
193. Identifying how tension is held.
194. Being detached from flow of action.
195. Having no goal but to be oneself.
196. Creation of role conflict.
197. Use of relaxation to produce extinction of fear response.
198. Formulating a question.
199. Asking a question.
200. Acting as if we knew answer to something that we don't understand.

CLUSTERS OF
COMPONENT STRATEGIES

LETTING GO

3. Allowing the action to evolve from the here and now situation.
32. Letting strategies arise from discrepancies in the here and now situation.
10. Making the least possible effort.
11. Physical nonresistance.
35. Allowing undesired behavior to extinguish itself through nonjudgmental reaction.
48. Release of body tension leading to release of the emotion bound in the tension.
50. Suspension of critical thinking.
51. Free associating of ideas, actions, emotions.
70. Regression (acting childish).
82. Letting go.
88. Allowing opportunity for integration of experience through relaxation.
123. Allowing the situation to remain unsolved.
175. Surrendering the illusion of personal unity created through possessing one body and one name.
195. Having no goal but to be oneself.

CONCRETIZING

5. Concretizing the abstract.
22. Making subjective experience objective.

248

89. Creating a physical expression of an emotional state.
105. Being aware of the physical setting as the basis of all action.
126. Feeling space (becoming physically aware of an abstract quality).
139. Becoming aware of how one feels in basic physical positions of lying, sitting, and standing.
148. Going through physical reorientation process after extended imagery experience.

VARIATION OF AN ELEMENT

2. Time allowed for session.
20. Sensory channels used for receiving perceptions.
21. Altering sensory input reaching a person.
30. Use of symbolic sensory stimuli (e.g., incense).
55. Use of substitute objects for carrying out forbidden acts (hitting a pillow instead of a person).
72. Conscious alteration of determinant of action (listening to tone of voice, not content).
138. Rapidly performing a number of different acts rather than staying with just one.
145. Switching strategies.
170. Acting in slow motion.
171. Separation of sexes for specific activities.
185. Putting things together not ordinarily related.

COMMUNICATIONS

1. Secrecy.
4. Interpretation of actions(e.g., psychoanalysis).
14. Use of touch as communications channel.
15. Use of touch as expression of affection and involvement.
26. Translating experience from one medium to another.
36. Expanding: (a) amount of communication available on given media, (b) number of media employed.
39. Control of communications network: (a) who talks to whom, (b) content, (c) order of communication.
44. Use of feedback (positive, negative, subjective, objective, past, present or future oriented).
60. Use of nonverbal communication to tap masked feelings.
103. Sharing experiences for mutual comfort.
109. Silence.
116. Attending not to what is said, but what is not said.
129. Talking about first impression.
167. Doing only what another individual requests.
175. Avoidance of negative statements.
183. Passing on what one has received.

188. Communicating with different selves.
190. Talking to others as if talking to oneself.
199. Asking a question.
200. Formulating a question.

ENERGY REDISTRIBUTION

23. Accumulating energy (e.g., through quiet breathing).
24. Redirecting group energy where most needed.
25. Completing a circuit of inner sensation.
47. Correction of internal imbalance through conscious intervention.
62. Displacement of tension downward (i.e., to cure headache).
66. Centering.
77. Continuing corrective action until energy system is rebalanced.
94. Relaxation through removal of tension from specific musical groups.
96. Relaxation through entering organic rhythms such as heart beat.
125. Changing physiological state through breathing, fasting, mortification, drugs.
133. Breathing according to conscious pattern.
135. Transformation of negative emotional energy to muscular energy.
147. Imaginal deconditioning.

HEIGHTENING PERSONAL INVOLVEMENT

49. Creating involvement for complete catharsis (verbal, nonverbal, imagery, action).
64. Utilization of personal problems as raw material for creative expression.
76. Personification of conflict (allowing each side to manifest).
98. Intensifying imagery flow.
127. Moving to music spontaneously and expressively.
156. Relating specific thoughts, emotions, actions and sensations to each other.

MANIPULATION

12. Breaking tension through physical intervention.
16. Changing behavior through alteration of imagery.
33. Rewarding desired behavior.
34. Punishing undesired behavior.
61. Alteration of group norms to force atypical actions from an individual.
78. Conscious suppression of particular behaviors (e.g., negative emotions).
107. Direct suggestion to change: (a) from self, (b) from others.
110. Relegation of authority from self to others.

187. Role playing.
197. Use of relaxation combined with fear stimuli to produce extinction of response.

TESTING THE LIMITS

7. Forcing the issue.
19. Redefining the nature of right and wrong behavior.
40. Role reversal.
181. Doing what we don't want to do.
68. Stopping vital functions (e.g., breathing, thought).
74. Creating an impossible situation to heighten or clarify relationships.
79. Acting in a new way in a given situation.
86. Practicing a symptom (e.g., stuttering).
111. Focusing on the avoided.
162. Creating shock by inappropriate behavior.
176. Accepting nothing.

MERGING WITH A COLLECTIVITY

18. Redefining the boundaries of the self.
53. Placing one's organism in the service of another.
102. Giving full attention to a supra-individual entity.
134. Focusing on moment of shift from in to out breathing as place where eternity enters time.

CONTROLLING ATTENTION

6. Splitting attention.
9. Enhancing awareness through the use of flowing movement.
38. Focusing attention where living action is occurring.
69. Focusing attention on given object.
95. Relaxation through directing attention around the body.
121. Establishing point of concentration (as in theater games).
106. Remembering self in the midst of action.
157. Doing a task while focusing on specific sensations.
192. Becoming aware you are causing tension.
193. Identifying how tension is held.
194. Standing aside, not submerging in flow of experience.

PROBLEM SOLVING

27. Keeping a journal.
28. Making specific efforts at certain times of day.
29. Utilization of ego ideal as motivation for action.
54. Using memory to integrate new experiences.

65. Use of guide, guru, or teacher.
91. Maintenance of independence in the helping relationship: (a) through scientific model (co-investigators), (b) self-help model (co-participants).
142. Returning periodically to a problem.
143. Use of imagery for problem solving.
168. Making a public commitment.
178. Having a clearly defined aim.
179. Struggling.

ENHANCEMENT OF CREATIVITY

37. Redefining a situation so that it becomes unique or unusual.
92. Improvising of situations, persons and objects.
99. Utilization of creative experience as a means of facing painful situation.
110. Use of analogies (personalize, direct, symbolic, fantasy).
124. Brainstorming.
130. Group fantasy.
186. Portraying own inner world.
190. Act as if you knew answer to something about which you are ignorant.

SELF IMAGE ALTERATION

115. Objectifying subjective determinants of person's world view.
182. Learning about self from watching one's reactions to others.
92. Creating and enacting new roles.

ENVIRONMENTAL ALTERATION

17. Changing behavior through environmental alteration.
90. Alteration of group composition.
91. Creating growth setting (strong environment, variety of possible settings, cultural island).
104. Suspending of basic assumptions about reality.

COMPONENT ACTIONS

secreting
timing
planning
connecting
concretizing
splitting
forcing
spreading
flowing
making least effort
nonresisting
intervening
touching
imaging
altering
redefining
eliminating
accumulating
completing
translating
recording
modeling
symbolizing
punishing
extinguishing
expanding
focusing

controlling
mirroring
imitating
reflecting
contrasting
going against
feeding back
expressing
releasing
involving
suspending
free associating
warming
giving
integrating
substituting
persisting
frustrating
nonverbal expressing
projecting
emerging
rewarding
rehearsing
utilizing
guiding
centering
moving

stopping
reversing
regressing
creating
locating
dissolving
paradoxing
limiting
personifying
continuing
doubling
suppressing
believing
self-actualizing
motivating
testing
deciding
choosing
practicing
pretending
pooling
displacing
suspending
physicalizing
suggesting
suspending
silencing
analyzing
relegating
paying
staying
approaching
testing
acting
goal setting
identifying
assuming
contacting
coaching
enacting
listening
concentrating
allowing
breathing
opening
pushing

improvising
distancing
relaxing
heightening
sharing
sensing
moving
encountering
utilizing
fantasizing
bombarding
rocking
stretching
lifting
passing
composing
reliving
transforming
objectifying
subjectifying
preparing
involving
expressing
performing
experiencing
lying
sitting
pulling
symbolizing
becoming
directing
balancing
closing
folding
unfolding
letting
aiding
chanting
singing
shrieking
fighting
moaning
solving
associating
switching
repeating

extracting
alternating
noting
undoing
reorienting
playing
speaking
splitting
standing
running
walking
swinging
turning
counteracting
reading
writing
transcribing
initiating
detecting
nonexpressing
entering
leaving

using
developing
suffering
committing
shifting
mismatching
formulating
relating
observing
taking
slowing
speeding
waiting
anticipating
emphasizing
falling
rising
contacting
avoiding
seeking
diagnosing
redirecting

NOTES AND REFERENCES

PREFACE

1. Dennison, G. *The Lives of Children* (New York: Random House, 1969).
   Faust, C. H. and Feingold, J., eds., *Approaches to Education for Charac-ter: Strategies for Change in Higher Education* (New York: Columbia University Press, 1969).
   Gross, R. and Gross, B., EDS., *Radical School Reform* (New York: Simon & Schuster, 1970).
   Hirsch, W. Z. and colleagues, *Inventing Education for the Future* (San Francisco, Chandler Pub., 1967).
   Kohl, H. R., *The Open Classroom* (New York: Review/Vintage, 1970).
   Leonard, G., *Education and Ecstasy* (New York: Delacorte, 1968).
   Rogers, V. R., *Teaching in the British Primary School* (New York: Mac-millan, 1970).
   Postman, N. and Weingartner, C., *Teaching as a Subversive Activity* (New York: Delacorte, 1969).
   Scribner, H. B., *Vermont Design for Education* (New York: Scribners, 1971).
   Big Rock Candy Mountain, Portola Institute, Menlo Park, California, 1970.
   Jones, R. M., *Fantasy and Feeling in Education* (New York: Harper & Row, 1970).
2. Virtually every national magazine has carried articles on the human po-tential movement of which growth centers are the most visible embodi-ment. See for example:
   Howard, Jane, "Inhibitions Thrown to the Gentle Wind," *Life*, July 12, 1968, pp. 48–65.
   "The Group: Joy on Thursday," *Newsweek*, May 12, 1969.
   "The New Eden," *Time*, October 3, 1969, pp. 45–47.
   Gross, Amy, "Getting Together," *Mademoiselle*, May 1970, pp. 154–206.
3. Borton, Terry, *Reach, Touch and Teach: Student Concerns and Process Education* (New York: McGraw-Hill, 1970).
4. Brown, George, *Human Teaching for Human Learning* (New York: Vi-king, 1971).

256

CHAPTER ONE

1. Selver, Charlotte, in conjunction with Brooks, V. W., "Report on Work in Sensory Awareness and Total Functioning," in *Explorations in Human Potentialities*, Herbert A. Otto, ed. (Springfield, Ill.: Thomas, 1966), pp. 487–504.
2. Gunther, Bernard, *Sense Relaxation* (New York: Collier, 1969) and *What to do Until the Messiah Comes* (New York: Collier, 1971).
3. R. O. Ballou, ed., *The Bible of the World* (New York: Viking, 1939), pp. 245–46.

CHAPTER TWO

1. The Optokinetic Perceptive Learning Device is being developed by Eleanor Criswell as a means of enhancing perceptual awareness and evolving consciousness. She is currently offering workshops at the Aureon Institute, New York City, on these applications of the device.
2. Sadhu, Mouni, *Concentration* (New York: Harper, 1959).
3. White, Minor, "Extended Perception through Photography and Suggestion," in *Ways of Growth*, Herbert A. Otto and John Mann, eds. (New York: Grossman, 1968), pp. 34–48.

CHAPTER THREE

1. Laban, Rudolph, *The Mastery of Movement* (London: MacDonald & Evans, 1960).

CHAPTER FOUR

1. See, for example, Krathwohl, D. R., Bloom, B. S. and Masia, B. B., *Taxonomy of Educational Objectives*, vol. II, The Affective Domain (New York: McKay, 1964).
2. Pearls, Frederick S., Hefferline, Ralph F. and Goodman, P., *Gestalt Therapy* (New York: Julian Press, 1962).
3. Kelly, George A., *The Psychology of Personal Constructs* (New York: Norton, 1955).
4. Bindrim, Paul, "Facilitating Peak Experiences," in *Ways of Growth*, Herbert A. Otto and John Mann, eds. (New York: Grossman, 1968), pp. 115–27.

CHAPTER FIVE

1. Hinton, C. H., *A New Era of Thought* (London, Sonnenschein, 1900).

CHAPTER SIX

1. Cline, V. B., and Richards, J. M., Jr., "Accuracy of Interpersonal Perception—a General Trait?", *J. abnorm. soc. Psychol.*, 1960, *60*, 1–7.

CHAPTER SEVEN

1. Ophiel, *The Art and Practice of Astral Projection* (San Francisco: Peach, 1967).
2. Rhine, J. B., *Extra-Sensory Perception* (Somerville, Mass. Humphries, 1962).
3. Pratt, J. G., Rhine, J. B., Smith, B. M., Stuart, C. E. and Greenwood, J. A., *Extra-Sensory Perception after Sixty Years* (New York: Holt, 1940).

CHAPTER EIGHT

1. A discussion of this point can be found in Mann, J., *Frontiers of Psychology* (Macmillan: New York, 1963), pp. 164–66.
2. Brown, G., "The Creative Sub-Self," in *Ways of Growth*, Herbert A. Otto and John Mann, eds. (New York: Grossman, 1968), pp. 147–57.
3. Parnes, Sidney J., *Creative Behavior Workbook* and *Creative Behavior Guidebook* (New York: Scribners, 1967).
4. Gordon, W. J., *Synectics* (New York: Collier, 1961).

CHAPTER NINE

1. Guilford, J. P., "The Structure of Intellect," *Psychol. Bull.*, 1956, *53*, pp. 267–93.

CHAPTER TEN

1. Trevitt, Virginia, *The American Heritage—Design for National Character* (Chicago: Rand-McNally, 1964).
2. Sorenson, R. and Dimock, H. S., *Designing Education in Valves* (New York: Association Press, 1955).
3. Ligon, Ernest M., *Dimensions of Character* (New York: Macmillan, 1956).

CHAPTER ELEVEN

1. James, David, ed., *Outward Bound* (London: Routledge, 1964).
2. Low, Abraham A., *Mental Health Through Will-Training* (Boston: Christopher, 1952).
3. Assagioli, Roberto, *Psychosynthesis* (New York: Hobbs Dorman, 1965).

CHAPTER TWELVE

1. Brunton, Paul, *The Wisdom of the Overself* (New York: Dutton, 1949).

CHAPTER THIRTEEN

1. Moreno, J. L., *Psychodrama*, Vol. 1 (New York: Beacon House, 1946), Sections 4 and 6.
2. Spolin, Viola, *Improvizations for the Theater* (Evanston: Northwestern University Press, 1963).

CHAPTER FOURTEEN

1. Skinner, B. F., *Walden Two* (New York: Macmillan, 1948).
2. Maltz, Maxwell, *Psychocybernetics* (Englewood Cliffs: Prentice-Hall, 1960).

CHAPTER SEVENTEEN

1. Leonard, George, *Education and Ecstasy* (New York: Delacorte, 1968).

APPENDIXES: *The Research Study on Strategies for Cultivating Human Potential*

1. The Appendixes material was developed when the author was a Consultant to the Educational Policy Research Center of the Stanford Research Institute. This Center is directed by Dr. Willis W. Harman and is sponsored by a continuing grant from the U. S. Office of Education. In the particular project to which the author was related approximately fifty methods for the release of human potentialities were reviewed and analyzed. Other members of the project team included Robert Mogar, Claudio Naranjo, and Severin Peterson.

APPENDIX ONE: STUDYING BEHAVIORAL STRATEGIES

1. Other sources were identified but not analyzed. These include the following:
   Pearls, F., Hefferline, R. F., and Goodman, P. *Gestalt Therapy* (New York: Dell, 1951).
   Otto, H. A., *Group Methods to Actualize Human Potential: A Handbook,* (mimeo), 1967.
   Spolin, Viola, *Improvization for the Theater* (Evanston: Northwestern University Press, 1963).
   Reps, P. S., *Zen Flesh—Zen Bones* (Rutland, Vermont: Tuttle, 1957).
   Malamud, D. I., and Machover, S., *Toward Self Understanding: Group Techniques in Self-Confrontation* (Springfield, Ill.: Thomas, 1965).
   Brunton, P., *Hidden Teaching Beyond Yoga* (New York: Dutton, 1942).

2. Huxley, L. A., *You Are Not the Target* (Farrar, Straus and Giroux, 1963).
3. Moore, S., *The Stanislavski System* (New York, Viking, 1965), pp. 25–30.
4. Mann, J., *Experiments On Myself*, (in manuscript).
5. Spolin, Viola, *Improvization for the Theater* (Evanston: Northwestern University Press, 1963), pp. 21–26.
6. Rolf, Ida, "Structural Reintegration," *Systematics, 1*, 1963, 3–20.
7. Schutz, W. C., *Joy* (New York: Grove, 1967).
8. *The Secret of the Golden Flower*, translated and explained, Wilhelm, R. (New York: Harcourt Brace, 1962).
9. Assagioli, R., *Psychosynthesis: A Manual of Principles and Techniques* (New York: Hobbs, 1965).
10. Otto, H. A., *Guide to Developing Your Potential* (New York: Scribners, 1967).
11. Gurdieff, G. I., *All and Everything* (Harcourt Brace, 1950).
12. Mann, J., *Changing Human Behavior* (New York, Scribners, 1965).
13. Tukey, J. W., "Comparing Individual Means in the Analysis of Variance," *Biometrics*, 1949, *5*, pp. 99–114.

Index

INDEX

overt behavior as approach to study of, 17–19
spontaneous action as approach to study of, 17, 18
as vehicle for self-understanding, 17, 18
Multicolored cube for developing visualization, 33, 34

Negative feedback, 232–239
Nonjudgmental approach to sensory awareness, 3–4
Nonresistance, 207

Objective feedback, 232–239
Operations, intelligence measuring, 66, 67
Ophiel, 49, 50, 53, 92
Outward Bound movement, 76
Outward Bound Program of Survival Training, 81–82

Pain for will training, 80–82
Paranormal abilities, 47–54
applications of, 51–52
astral projection as, 92
defined, 49
method, 49–51
class in, 52–54
climate of opinion about, 47–48
Parnes, Sidney, 57
Past, reliving, for meditation, 91
Peak-oriented psychotherapy, 27–28
Perception, defined, 14
Perceptual awareness, 11–16
applications of, 14–15
class in, 15–16
Personal involvement, heightening, 250

Personality theories, pleasure maximization in most, 102
Photographs, four stages of perception of, 13–14
Physical education, movement and, 17; see also Movement
Positive feedback, 232–239
Positive reconditioning in behavior therapy, 105
Power structures, types of, 232–239
Pratt, J. G., 54
Prescott College, 82
Principles
general, in component strategy training, 133, 135–136
resocializing, 104–106
translation principle, 16
Products, intelligence measuring, 66, 67
Psychoanalysis, 27, 129
Psychocybernetics, 109
Psychosynthesis, 77–78
Psychotherapy
component strategy in, 132
dynamic, for emotional reeducation, 24–27
reorganizing individual life space in, 112–113
time orientation in, 203
Punishment in conditioning, 103–104

Raja Yoga, 83, 90
Reading people
empathy and, 42
insufficiency of, 46
Reciprocal inhibition, 105
Redefining, 209